First World War
and Army of Occupation
War Diary
France, Belgium and Germany

41 DIVISION
123 Infantry Brigade,
Brigade Machine Gun Company
17 June 1916 - 31 October 1917

WO95/2639/4

The Naval & Military Press Ltd
www.nmarchive.com
Published in association with The National Archives

Published by

The Naval & Military Press Ltd

Unit 10 Ridgewood Industrial Park,

Uckfield, East Sussex,

TN22 5QE England

Tel: +44 (0) 1825 749494

www.naval-military-press.com

www.nmarchive.com

This diary has been reprinted in facsimile from the original. Any imperfections are inevitably reproduced and the quality may fall short of modern type and cartographic standards.

© Crown Copyright
Images reproduced by permission of The National Archives, London, England, 2015.

Contents

Document type	Place/Title	Date From	Date To
Heading	WO95/2639/4		
Heading	41st Division 123rd Infy Bde 123rd Machine Gun Coy. Jun 1916-1917 Oct.		
Heading	War Diary Of 123 M G Coy. from 17.6.16 to 31.7.16 Volume I		
War Diary	Le Bizet	24/06/1916	06/07/1916
War Diary	Grantham	17/06/1916	17/06/1916
War Diary	Southampton	17/06/1916	17/06/1916
War Diary	Havre	18/06/1916	19/06/1916
War Diary	Steenwerck Pont De Nieppe Le Bizet	20/06/1916	23/06/1916
War Diary	Le Bizet	07/07/1916	31/07/1916
Heading	War Diary 123rd Machine Gun Company From 1st August-31 August 1916 Volume I		
War Diary	Le Bizet Zy Front	01/08/1916	17/08/1916
War Diary	Mont Des Cats.	17/08/1916	20/08/1916
War Diary	R 31 B 5.2 27 1/40000	21/08/1916	22/08/1916
War Diary	Bailleul	23/08/1916	31/08/1916
War Diary	Ergnies	01/09/1916	06/09/1916
War Diary	Becoudel	07/09/1916	08/09/1916
War Diary	Fillcourt	09/09/1916	09/09/1916
War Diary	Montauban	10/09/1919	17/09/1919
War Diary	Becoudel	18/09/1916	27/09/1916
War Diary	Manzaugan	27/09/1916	01/10/1916
War Diary	Montauban	01/10/1916	03/10/1916
War Diary	Mametz Wood	04/10/1916	06/10/1916
War Diary	In The Line	07/10/1916	10/10/1916
War Diary	Mametz Wood	11/10/1916	12/10/1916
War Diary	Dernacourt	13/10/1916	17/10/1916
War Diary	Frucourt	18/10/1916	19/10/1916
War Diary	Godewaersvelde	20/10/1916	21/10/1916
War Diary	Chippewa Camp	22/10/1916	22/10/1916
War Diary	In The Line	23/10/1916	26/10/1916
War Diary	In The Field	27/10/1916	31/10/1916
War Diary	Reninghelst	01/11/1916	02/11/1916
War Diary	Voormezeele	03/11/1916	08/11/1916
War Diary	Chippewa Camp	09/11/1916	15/11/1916
War Diary	Voormezeele	16/11/1916	22/11/1916
War Diary	Quebec Camp	23/11/1916	27/11/1916
War Diary	Voormezeele	28/11/1916	30/11/1916
Operation(al) Order(s)	Operation Order No. 1 by Captain C. F. Dingwall Commanding 123rd Machine Gun Company.	01/11/1916	01/11/1916
Operation(al) Order(s)	Operation Orders No. 1 By Capt. C. F. Dingwall Commanding 123rd Machine Gun Coy.		
Miscellaneous	Operation Order II by Capt C. F. Dingwall Commanding 123rd M G. Coy.	14/11/1916	14/11/1916
Operation(al) Order(s)	Operation Orders No.3 by Captain C. F. Dingwall Commanding 123rd Machine Gun Company	21/11/1916	21/11/1916
Operation(al) Order(s)	Operation Order 4 by Capt C. F. Dingwall Commanding 123rd M.G. Coy.	24/11/1916	24/11/1916

Type	Description	Start	End
Operation(al) Order(s)	Operation Order No. 5 By Capt. C. F. Dingwall Commanding 123rd Machine Gun Coy	26/11/1916	26/11/1916
Miscellaneous	123rd Infantry Brigade. Summary Of Casualties During Month Of November, 1916		
War Diary	Voormezeele	01/12/1916	02/12/1916
War Diary	Quebec Camp Reninghelst	03/12/1916	08/12/1916
War Diary	Voormezeele	09/12/1916	14/12/1916
War Diary	Reninghelst	15/12/1916	21/12/1916
War Diary	Voormezeele	22/12/1916	28/12/1916
War Diary	Reninghelst	29/12/1916	31/12/1916
Miscellaneous	O.C. 123rd. M.G. Coy.	31/12/1916	31/12/1916
Operation(al) Order(s)	Operation Orders No. 6 by Captain C. F. Dingwall, commanding 123rd M.G. Coy.	01/12/1916	01/12/1916
Operation(al) Order(s)	Operation Order No. 7 by Captain C. F. Dingwall, Commanding 123 M.G. Company.	04/12/1916	04/12/1916
Operation(al) Order(s)	Operation Order 8 by Captain C. F. Dingwall Commanding 123rd Machine Gun Company.	06/12/1916	06/12/1916
Operation(al) Order(s)	Operation Orders 9 By Lieut. S. Scott. Commanding 123rd Machine Gun Company.	12/12/1916	12/12/1916
Operation(al) Order(s)	Operation Order 10 by Lt. S. Scott Commdg 123rd Machine Gun Company.	15/12/1916	15/12/1916
Operation(al) Order(s)	Operation Orders 11 by Lieut. S. Scott. Commanding 123rd Machine Gun Company.	20/12/1916	20/12/1916
Operation(al) Order(s)	Operation Order 12 by Captain C. F. Dingwall commanding 123rd Machine Gun Company.	27/12/1916	27/12/1916
Operation(al) Order(s)	Operation Orders 13 by Captain C. F. Dingwall Commanding 123rd Machine Gun Company.	30/12/1916	30/12/1916
War Diary	Reninghelst	01/01/1917	01/01/1917
War Diary	Voormezeele	02/01/1917	06/01/1917
War Diary	Reninghelst	07/01/1917	13/01/1917
War Diary	Voormezeele	14/01/1917	20/01/1917
War Diary	Reninghelst	21/01/1917	26/01/1917
War Diary	Voormezeele	27/01/1917	31/01/1917
Operation(al) Order(s)	Operation Orders No. 14 by Captain C. F. Dingwall Commanding 123rd Machine Gun Company	01/01/1917	01/01/1917
Operation(al) Order(s)	Operation Orders 15 By Captain C. F. Dingwall Commanding 123rd Machine Gun Company.	06/01/1917	06/01/1917
Operation(al) Order(s)	Operation Orders 16 by Captain C. F. Dingwall Commanding 123rd Machine Gun Company	09/01/1917	09/01/1917
Operation(al) Order(s)	Operation Orders. 17 by Captain C. F. Dingwall Commanding 123rd Machine Gun Company	11/01/1917	11/01/1917
Operation(al) Order(s)	Operation Orders 18 by Captain C. F. Dingwall commanding 123rd Machine Gun Company.	20/01/1917	20/01/1917
Operation(al) Order(s)	Operation Orders 19 by Captain C. F. Dingwall, commanding 123rd Machine Gun Company.	23/01/1917	23/01/1917
Operation(al) Order(s)	Operation Orders 20 by captain C. F. Dingwall Commanding 123rd Machine Gun Company.	26/01/1917	26/01/1917
War Diary	Voormezeele	01/02/1917	01/02/1917
War Diary	Reninghelst	02/02/1917	08/02/1917
War Diary	Voormezeele	09/02/1917	15/02/1917
War Diary	Reninghelst	16/02/1917	20/02/1917
War Diary	Voormezeele	21/02/1917	25/02/1917
War Diary	Reninghelst	26/02/1917	28/02/1917
Operation(al) Order(s)	Operation Order 21 by Captain C. F. Dingwall, Commanding 123rd Machine Gun Company.	31/01/1917	31/01/1917

Type	Description	Start	End
Operation(al) Order(s)	Operation Orders 22, by Captain C. F. Dingwall, Commanding 123rd Machine Gun Company.	04/02/1917	04/02/1917
Operation(al) Order(s)	Operation Orders. No. 23 by Capt C. F. Dingwall commanding 123rd Machine Gun Company.	07/02/1917	07/02/1917
Operation(al) Order(s)	Operation Order No. 24 by Captain C. F. Dingwall Commanding 123rd Machine Gun Company.	15/02/1917	15/02/1917
Operation(al) Order(s)	Operation Order 25 by Captain C. F. Dingwall Commanding 123rd Machine Gun Company.	18/02/1917	18/02/1917
Operation(al) Order(s)	Operation Order 26 by Captain C. F. Dingwall Commanding 123rd Machine Gun Company.	20/02/1917	20/02/1917
Operation(al) Order(s)	Operation Orders 27 by Major C. F. Dingwall Commanding 123rd Machine Gun Company.	25/02/1917	25/02/1917
War Diary	Reninghelst	01/03/1917	03/03/1917
War Diary	Voormezeele	04/03/1917	09/03/1917
War Diary	Reninghelst	10/03/1917	15/03/1917
War Diary	Voormezeele	16/03/1917	21/03/1917
War Diary	Reninghelst	22/03/1917	28/03/1917
War Diary	Voormezeele	29/03/1917	31/03/1917
Operation(al) Order(s)	Operation Orders 28 by Major C. F. Dingwall Commanding 123rd Machine Gun Company.	01/03/1917	01/03/1917
Operation(al) Order(s)	Operation Orders 29N by Major C. F. Dingwall Commanding 123rd Machine Gun Company.	03/03/1917	03/03/1917
Operation(al) Order(s)	Operation Orders 30 by Major C. F. Dingwall, commanding 123rd Machine Gun Company.	07/03/1917	07/03/1917
Operation(al) Order(s)	Operation Order 31 by Major C. F. Dingwall commanding 123rd Machine Gun Company.	09/03/1917	09/03/1917
Operation(al) Order(s)	Operation Orders 32 by Major C. F. Dingwall Commanding 123rd Machine Gun Company.	12/03/1917	12/03/1917
Operation(al) Order(s)	Operation Order No. 33 by Major C. F. Dingwall commanding 123rd Machine Gun Company.	14/03/1917	14/03/1917
Operation(al) Order(s)	Operation Order No. 34 by Major C. F. Dingwall, Commanding 123rd Machine Gun Company.	21/03/1917	21/03/1917
Operation(al) Order(s)	Operation Order 35 by Major C. F. Dingwall, Commanding 123rd Machine Gun Company.	24/03/1917	24/03/1917
Operation(al) Order(s)	Operation Orders No. 36 by Major C. F. Dingwall commanding 123rd Machine Gun Company	27/03/1917	27/03/1917
War Diary	Voormezeele.	01/04/1917	03/04/1917
War Diary	Micmac	04/04/1917	05/04/1917
War Diary	On March	06/04/1917	08/04/1917
War Diary	Hellebroucq	09/04/1917	10/04/1917
War Diary	Pas de Calais	11/04/1917	22/04/1917
War Diary	On March	23/04/1917	25/04/1917
War Diary	Reninghelst Quebec Camp	26/04/1917	30/04/1917
Miscellaneous	March Orders (Operation Order 40) by Major C. F. Dingwall Commdg 123rd Coy, M.G. Corps.	22/04/1917	22/04/1917
Miscellaneous	March Orders by Major C. F. Dingwall Commanding 123rd Machine Gun Company. No. 39	05/04/1917	05/04/1917
Operation(al) Order(s)	Operation Orders 38 by Major C. F. Dingwall Commanding 123rd Machine Gun Company.	03/04/1917	03/04/1917
Operation(al) Order(s)	Operation Orders No. 37 by Major C. F. Dingwall commanding 123rd Machine Gun Company.	03/04/1916	03/04/1916
War Diary	Reninghelst	01/04/1917	02/04/1917
War Diary	Voormezeele	03/04/1917	20/04/1917
War Diary	Reninghelst	21/04/1917	26/04/1917
War Diary	Yoormigeele	27/04/1917	01/06/1917

Miscellaneous	Operation Orders by Lieut S. Scott. Commanding 123rd Coy. M.G. Corps. (No. 41)		
Operation(al) Order(s)	Operation Orders 43, by Lieut S. Scott, commanding 123rd Machine Gun Company.	18/05/1917	18/05/1917
Operation(al) Order(s)	Operation Orders 45 by Major C. F. Dingwall commanding 123rd Machine Gun Company.	24/05/1917	24/05/1917
War Diary	Reninghelst	01/06/1917	23/06/1917
War Diary	Voormezeele	24/06/1917	30/06/1917
Operation(al) Order(s)	Operation Orders 48 by Lieut A. Mc. K. Reid, commanding 123rd Machine Gun Company.	04/05/1917	04/05/1917
Operation(al) Order(s)	Operation Order No. 46, by Major C. F. Dingwall, commanding 123rd Machine Gun Company.	30/05/1917	30/05/1917
Miscellaneous	123rd Machine Gun Company.	31/05/1917	31/05/1917
Map			
Miscellaneous	Message		
Operation(al) Order(s)	Operation Orders 49 by Lieut. S. Scott. commanding 123rd Machine Gun Company.	19/06/1917	19/06/1917
Operation(al) Order(s)	Operation Orders 50 by Lieut. S. Scott, commanding 123rd Coy, M.G. Corps.	23/06/1917	23/06/1917
Operation(al) Order(s)	Operation Order 51 by Lieut A. McK. Reid., commanding 123rd Machine Gun Company.	27/06/1917	27/06/1917
War Diary	Old French Trench	01/07/1917	01/07/1917
War Diary	Murrumbidgee Camp	02/07/1917	02/07/1917
War Diary	Thieushook	03/07/1917	21/07/1917
War Diary	Westoutre	22/07/1917	31/07/1917
Operation(al) Order(s)	Operation Orders 52 by Lieut. A. McK. Reid, M.C. Commanding 123rd Coy, M.G. Corps.	30/06/1917	30/06/1917
Operation(al) Order(s)	Operation (March) Orders 53 by Lieut A. McK. Reid, MC commanding 123rd Coy. M.G. Corps.	01/07/1917	01/07/1917
Operation(al) Order(s)	Operation Orders (March) 54 By Captain A McReid, M.C. Commanding 123 Coy M.G.C.	20/07/1917	20/07/1917
War Diary	Bluff Sector	01/08/1917	11/08/1917
War Diary	Meteren	12/08/1917	19/08/1917
War Diary	Staples	20/08/1917	20/08/1917
War Diary	Esquerdes	22/08/1917	13/09/1917
War Diary	Staple	14/09/1917	14/09/1917
War Diary	Meleren	15/09/1917	15/09/1917
War Diary	Reninghelst	16/09/1917	17/09/1917
War Diary	Ridge Wood	18/09/1917	19/09/1917
War Diary	Shrewsbury Forest	20/09/1917	26/09/1917
War Diary	Reninghelst	27/09/1917	29/09/1917
War Diary	Bray Dunes	30/09/1917	04/10/1917
War Diary	Coxyde Bains	05/10/1917	06/10/1917
War Diary	Nieuport Bains Sector	07/10/1917	14/10/1917
War Diary	Coxyde Bains	14/10/1917	14/10/1917
War Diary	La Panne	15/10/1917	31/10/1917

WO95/26529 (A)

WO95/26539 (A)

41ST DIVISION
123RD INFY BDE

123RD MACHINE GUN COY.

JUN 1916 – ~~FEB 1918~~ 1917 OCT

To ITALY

JUNE
JULY

41

123 M.G. Coy
Vols 1·2

Confidential

War Diary
of
123 M G Coy

From 17.VI.1916 to 31.VII.1916

Volume I

June '16
Feb '18

Army Form C. 2

WAR DIARY
or
INTELLIGENCE SUMMARY
(Erase heading not required.)

Instructions regarding War Diaries and Intelligence Summaries are contained in F.S. Regs., Part II. and the Staff Manual respectively. Title Pages will be prepared in manuscript.

Place	Date	Hour	Summary of Events and Information	Remarks and references to Appendices
LE. BIZET	June 24		Took over Sector from 4th M.G. Squadron. Relief Completed. AA	
	26		4th M.G. Squadron Left. AA	
	27 } 28 }		Trench routine. Hostile M.Gs active	
	29	7 AM	R.F.A. wire cutting. Raid at 11pm on enemy trenches by infantry. Moderate hostile retaliation. Machine guns active on flanks	
	30		Trench routine. M.Gs active at night. One rank & file wounded	
July	1		Quiet. Gun No 4117 Struck by a Stray bullet through Barrel Casing. AA	
	2		Quiet. Artillery active	
	3		Quiet. M.Gs active at night	
	4		Warm & bright. Hostile M.Gs active from parapet at night	
	5		Traversing & elevating chiefs arrived. Warm.	
	6		Artillery more active. M.Gs active at night. Indirect Fire result unobserved. AA	

WAR DIARY
or
INTELLIGENCE SUMMARY
(Erase heading not required.)

Army Form C. 2118.

Instructions regarding War Diaries and Intelligence Summaries are contained in F.S. Regs., Part II. and the Staff Manual respectively. Title Pages will be prepared in manuscript.

Place	Date	Hour	Summary of Events and Information	Remarks and references to Appendices
GRANTHAM	17.VI	AM 4.40	Entrained at Military Dock GRANTHAM	
SOUTHAMPTON		PM 1.5	Detrained at SOUTHAMPTON	
		5.30pm	Embarked on board Transport CASSAREA (Personnel) and BELLEROPHON (Transport)	
HAVRE	18 VI	4.30am	Arrived at HAVRE.	
		7.30am	Disentrained	
		5 pm	Marched to No I Rest Camp	
	19th	10.50am	Departed from No I Rest Camp	
		1.15pm	Entrained at GARE des MARCHANDISES	
STEENWERCK	20th	1.30pm	Detrained at STEENWERCK	
But de NIEPPE		4.0pm	Reported at 123 Brigade HQ	
LE BIZET		5.15pm	Arrived at LE BIZET.	
	21st	6.0pm	G.O.C. 41st Division inspected the Company in Nieppe	
	22nd		2/Lieuts O.T GIBBONS, M.A. BEATON & 25 other ranks moved to the Trenches.	
			32 other Ranks GOEPEL, PAYNE, MACINTOSH, FAWCETT, REID moved to the Trenches	
	23rd		Remainder of Company moved up. 2/Lieut SCOTT moved up	

WAR DIARY

INTELLIGENCE SUMMARY

(Erase heading not required.)

Army Form C. 2118.

Instructions regarding War Diaries and Intelligence Summaries are contained in F.S. Regs., Part II and the Staff Manual respectively. Title Pages will be prepared in manuscript.

Place	Date	Hour	Summary of Events and Information	Remarks and references to Appendices
LE BIZET	July 7	—	Quiet. M.gs active at night. Buiet has Gun emplacements consolidated. Hostile M.gs particularly active opposite Salient. Indirect Fire	
	8	—	Intermittent Artillery Fire. 2/Lieut FAWCETT wounded in F102 by Sniper. Hostile M.gs active at night.	
	9	—	Reliefs Inter-Company. Indirect Fire on DEULÉMONT ROAD. LE BIZET Shelled. one other rank wounded.	
	10		Trench routine. Warm Indirect Fire on BLANCHISSERIE. Hostile M.Gs active at night. 2/Lieut. M.A. BEATON admitted to Hospital.	
	11		Spare parts arrived. Trench routine. Quiet & warm. LE BIZET Shelled Hostile M.gs active at night.	
	12		Quiet. NAPOO AVENUE emplacement completed. Warm. Indirect Fire M.gs very active at night.	
	13		Trench routine. Hostile M.gs active at night. Indirect Fire on LYS River Bridges. LE BIZET Shelled on both days. Hostile M.gs active at night	
	14			
	15		C.H.Q. bombarded from 7.52 - 8.34. C.S.M. WATT & one other rank wounded	
	16		Trench routine. Indirect Fire. Hot. LE BIZET Shelled M.gs active	
	17		One other rank returned to duty. Indirect Fire on FRELINGHIEN	
	18		LE BIZET Shelled. LANCASHIRE SUPPORT FARM Shelled Indirect Fire on FME DURIEZ	
	19		Indirect Fire on USINE & HALTE. Hostile M.gs quieter. Our M.gs active	

Army Form C. 2118.

WAR DIARY
or
INTELLIGENCE SUMMARY

(Erase heading not required.)

Place	Date	Hour	Summary of Events and Information	Remarks and references to Appendices
LE BIZET	July 20		Hostile M.gs now never fire from parapet & are not so active.	
	21		Hostile M.gs more than usually active. Indirect Fire on BLANCHISSERIE	
	22		Gun No 4117 damaged by Trench Mortar. Emplacement damaged	
	23		16 men joined. Temporarily attached. School commenced. Artillery duel. Enemy nervous at night. Indirect Fire on DÉULÉMONT ROAD.	
	24		One other rank killed. Enemy Trench Mortars easily lively. Indirect Fire & Fire During	
	25		Fine but dull. Thick mist at night. No hostile M.g fire. Indirect Fire on TWIN COTTAGES	
	26		Raid by 20th D.L.I Supported by M.g fire on flanks from T96 & T93. A heavy artillery duel.	
	27		Hot & fine. Quiet especially M.gs of enemy. Indirect Fire on FRELINGHIEN	
	28		Hot & fine. Working parts dispersed from T93. Indirect Fire on BLANCHISSERIE	
	29		Relief inter-company. Quiet warm & fine. Hostile working party driven in. 32 men joined from Brigade 16 permanently attached 16 temporarily attached	
	30		Very hot & sunny. Hostile M.g's did not fire at all. Indirect Fire on FRELINGHIEN	
	31		Very warm, particularly quiet especially at night. Indirect Fire on Pontoon Bridge	

41/123.MGC
VOL 4
3

Confidential.

Confidential
War Diary

123rd Machine Gun Company

From 1st August – 31 August 1916.

Volume I

Army Form C. 2118.

WAR DIARY
or
INTELLIGENCE SUMMARY
(Erase heading not required.)

Instructions regarding War Diaries and Intelligence Summaries are contained in F. S. Regs., Part II. and the Staff Manual respectively. Title Pages will be prepared in manuscript.

Place	Date	Hour	Summary of Events and Information	Remarks and references to Appendices
LE BIZET 2y Front	Aug 1st		Very Quiet. Hot & Sunny. Tested front line guns at night. Indirect Fire on BLANCHESSERIE. RR	
	2nd		Again Quiet. Hot & Sunny. M.G more active at night. Indirect Fire on HALTE. RR	
	3rd		Hostile artillery more lively. Hostile M.gs a shade more active. Rebound wire	
	4th		Trench Routine. Very quiet as regards M.gs. Work on wire. Glasgow redoubt & SUFFOLK AVENUE. Practised night firing. RR	
	5th			
	6th		Hostile M.gs extraordinarily quiet. Indirect fire on HALTE & DÉULÉMONT. Work on wire & new emplacements. RR	
	7th		Trench Routine. LE BIZET Shelled. RR	
	8th		Warm & Quiet. Indirect Fire on TRESLINGHEM. RR	
	9th		All Quiet. Indirect Fire from LYS FARM on BRIQUETERIE. RR	
	10th		All Quiet. Indirect fire on HALTE & Trench Tramway near TIN COTTAGES. RR	

WAR DIARY
or
INTELLIGENCE SUMMARY

(Erase heading not required.)

Army Form C. 2118

Place	Date	Hour	Summary of Events and Information	Remarks and references to Appendices
	11		Brigade M.G. School commenced at LA CRÈCHE. Sgt Porter & 10 men commenced Indirect Fire on TWIN COTTAGES. RRA	
	12		Hostile M.Gs appear to have been withdrawn. Very quiet at night. Suffolk Avenue Emplacement Indirect Fire on FREBINGHEIN. RRA	finishing ?
	13		Warned to prepare for relief. Hot. Very quiet at night. Building new emplacements at night	
	14/15		Indirect fire on BLANCHISSERIE Area. Brigade School closed. RRA Attc quiet & very warm. Arrived & commenced taking over. Building new emplacements at night	
			O.C. 18 Coy 1 O.R wounded. A.O.Rs. joined. Rain RRA	
			Hostile M.Gs did not fire at all. Moved to Transport Lines. Rain RRA	
	16		Handed over relief. Confined at 4.15 p.m. Moved to complete establishment. Handing over Satisfactory. RRA Drew 3 mules	
	17		Moved to R 31 B 6.2. near MONT DES CATS. Bivovacked. RRA Sheet 27	
MONT DES CATS.	18		Cleaning Parade. Kit inspection. Guns overhauled. Rained at intervals. Warm	
	19		Route March with leading exercise. Gun Drill etc. Mont Des Cats area.	RRA

Army Form C. 2118.

WAR DIARY
or
INTELLIGENCE SUMMARY

(Erase heading not required.)

Instructions regarding War Diaries and Intelligence Summaries are contained in F. S. Regs., Part II. and the Staff Manual respectively. Title Pages will be prepared in manuscript.

Place	Date	Hour	Summary of Events and Information	Remarks and references to Appendices
MONT DES CATS	Aug 20		Route March about 10½ miles. No one fell out. 1 Other rank joined. Tactical Exercise. Gun Drill. Guns overhauled.	
R31B52 27 ½/40,000	21		Route March via FLETRE. THIEUSHOOK. MONT DES CATS. About 13 miles. Tactical exercise. Guns overhauled.	
	22		Men bathed. Advanced Drill & Tactical problems for Officers. 4 Other ranks joined.	
BAILLEUL	23		Entrained at 6.30 A.M for PONT REMY. LONGPRES. Arrived PONT REMY LONGPRES 4.30 P.M. marched to ERGNIES village. Billets in 4th Army Area. GORENFLOS district. Training for the offensive & Tactical exercises. Weather fine. The need of a Field Cooker has been urgently felt & would seem to be necessary.	 31.8.16
24th to 31st				

Army Form C. 2118.

Vol 4
M.G.C
123/41

WAR DIARY
or
INTELLIGENCE SUMMARY

(Erase heading not required.)

Place	Date	Hour	Summary of Events and Information	Remarks and references to Appendices
ERQUIRES	1916 Sept 1 to 5 Sept 6		Tactical training with Brigade. Inspection by G.O.C Divisional Reft Engines to Hericourt arriving at 7.30pm	
BECORDEL	" 7		Camp of BECORDEL 1.30 A.M. 2 md Lt Kirkward reported to company	
	" 8		O.C. & 2/Lt Scott view of trenches in DEVIL WOOD area. Company under 2/Lt Reid holding position. 2/Lt Payne left to report to 87 M-G Coy. 2/Lt Gilbourn left to report to 101 M.G. Coy. Lt Thomas & 2/Lt Shaw reported to company	
FRICOURT	" 9		Moved to camp at FRICOURT	
MONTAUBAN	" 10		Company moved to MONTAUBAN. Sections 3 & 4 moved up to left section of line	
	" 11		Section 7 & 8 at 3.30 AM. moved up to right section of line. Remainder of company in reserve at company headquarters	
	" 12		Consolidating of line under company relief	
	" 13		Relieved by 162 company on left. 124 company on right. Encamped at POMMIER Redoubt. 123rd	
	" 14		Brigade in reserve to divisional move into position during the night 14/15. Sud Yeoman an officer detailed to lead battalion. Eight guns in reserve under M. Julien at CATERon TRENCH, four with battalion moved forward to own original front line during the afternoon, at 11pm they moved to a line south of FLERS	
	" 16		Company H.Q. and reserve guns moved forward to South of FLERS. Four with battalion taking up position on right flank of FLERS Counallies very slight. No firing by Germans	
	" 17		Guns still in same position, although heavily shelled. Capt Auchinleck & 2/Lt Gospel killed at 2.30pm 2/Lt W. As Intosh wounded. The Yeovily killed at 3pm other ranks wounded 13. During night of 17/18 company withdrawn from trenches	
BECORDEL	" 18		Move into camp at BECORDEL L.5/Sgt 13 men with 2guns & report failed to report but reported at 6pm on the 19th all but three men with one gun & lorpost	
	" 19 to 27		At rest at BECORDEL camp and reorganising company 2/Lt Kirkward acting O.C 2nd Lt Shaw joined 26th 2/Lt D.A. WAUGH joined company 24/9/16. Capt H. Royal and 2/Lt N.J.V. Hoover joined 26th inst	

Army Form C 2118.

WAR DIARY
or
INTELLIGENCE SUMMARY
(Erase heading not required.)

Instructions regarding War Diaries and Intelligence Summaries are contained in F. S. Regs., Part II. and the Staff Manual respectively. Title Pages will be prepared in manuscript.

Place	Date	Hour	Summary of Events and Information	Remarks and references to Appendices
Mantauban	1916 Sept 27		Moved into camp near Mantauban arriving 11 pm	
	28		Moved into the line to consolidate HQ at FLERS, line running just W of GUEUDECOURT to Factory Corner & Relieved by 36th M.g. Coy	
Oct 1				

Monk Capt
O.C. 123rd M.G. Coy

Army Form C. 2118

123 Machine Gun Coy.   Vol 5

WAR DIARY or INTELLIGENCE SUMMARY

(Erase heading not required.)

Instructions regarding War Diaries and Intelligence Summaries are contained in F. S. Regs., Part II. and the Staff Manual respectively. Title Pages will be prepared in manuscript.

Place	Date	Hour	Summary of Events and Information	Remarks and references to Appendices
MONTAUBAN	1/10/16		Relieved by the 36th M.G. Coy.	
	2/10/16		& return to Camp at MONTAUBAN.	
	3/10/16			
MAMETZ WOOD	4/10/16		Left MONTAUBAN for MAMETZ WOOD where Coy arrived about 11pm	
"	5/10/16		In Camp at MAMETZ WOOD	
"	6/10/16		Do.	
2nd Line	7/10/16		Left MAMETZ WOOD. Were Inverness Brown. 8 guns went forward with the Battalion. 2 to SWITCH TRENCH, 2 to SAVOY TRENCH & 2 to CIRTON TRENCH. Other 8 guns were in Reserve in YORK TRENCH.	
"	8/10/16		The Brigade made tremendous attack. Guns supported the forward guns.	
"	9/10/16		In the line somewhere.	
"	10/10/16		In the line somewhere. Relieved ammn the night by the 89th M.G. Coy.	
MAMETZ WOOD	11/10/16		In the line Company buried, relieved	
		5 P.M.	Relief completed. Company leaves to Camp at MAMETZ WOOD. Company & Mules don't get there before Sunrise fair.	
"	12/10/16		No Orders received.	
DERNANCOURT	13/10/16		Brigade moves to relieve to MEAULTE PAST and EDT. DERNANCOURT. by train	
			Time spent in instruction in Anti gas measures - Gun cleaning	
"	14/10/16		& Cleaning of the men.	
			Divisional General inspects the Brigade Released the debts Church Parade	
"	15/10/16		Transport moved off by Road to the 3rd Army Area	
	16/10/16		Made preparation for taking gun measured [to] the Company	

WAR DIARY
or
INTELLIGENCE SUMMARY

(Erase heading not required.)

Army Form C. 2118

Place	Date	Hour	Summary of Events and Information	Remarks and references to Appendices
BERNACOURT	17/10/16	12 Noon	Entrain at EDGE HILL Siding for GREAT NORTHERN for OISEMENT.	
OISEMENT	18/10/16	3.45 AM	Arrive OISEMENT and march away to Billets at	
		7.0 AM	AIRCOURT Billeted at the Chateau of Mme la Duchesse de Chaulu	
"	19/10/16	9 AM	Transport marching off the entrain at PONT REMY	
		2.30 PM	Company entraining at PONT REMY for GODEWAERSVELDE	
GODEWAERSVELDE	20/10/16	2 AM	Detrain at GODEWAERSVELDE & march to Billets	
"	21/10/16		Company Parades. Gun cleaning & Drill. Inspection - Anti gas measures.	
			Officers go on tour of inspection to St ELOI Relative	
CHIPPEWA CAMP	22/10/16		Company with transport moves to Huts at CHIPPEWA CAMP	
			near RENINGHELST	
On the Line	23/10/16		Company relieving 13 Rd Aust M.G. Coy in St FLOI Sector	
		8.0 AM	Leave Camp & March to Dickebusch	
		9.30 PM	Relief Complete	
"	24/10/16		Details just carried out during preceding nt.	
			Day time spent in improving Gun Positions and Dugouts	
			Some rain experienced but much trench	
"	25/10/16		Consolidation and Improvement.	
"	26/10/16		Officers 135 Rd M.G. Coy came to look over the line - Preparatory	
			Relief	

Army Form C. 21

WAR DIARY
or
INTELLIGENCE SUMMARY

(Erase heading not required.)

Instructions regarding War Diaries and Intelligence Summaries are contained in F. S. Regs., Part II. and the Staff Manual respectively. Title Pages will be prepared in manuscript.

Place	Date	Hour	Summary of Events and Information	Remarks and references to Appendices
In Field	27/10/16		Further improvement & consolidation carried on positions. Reliefs (two officers of 122nd M.G. Coy) are to be carried out tonight.	
	28/10/16	11.7pm	Company relieved by 122nd M.G. Coy.	
		3.30pm	Relief commenced. Relief complete.	
			Company marched to 6 CHIPPEWA CAMP. CHIPPEWA CAMP under European phivels. Company moved into KINORA CAMP.	
	29/10/16		Returned to then at RENINGHELST.	
	30/10/16	3.10pm	Company moved back to CHIPPEWA CAMP — no improvements whatever. Company in Rest.	
	31/10/16		Company in Rest. Day spent in fitting and issuing much to thing. General cleaning up for Army Commander's Inspection on the first of November.	

W. Spooner B?, O. Coy
123 R.D.? M.S. Coy

123rd Machine Gun Company
WAR DIARY
or
INTELLIGENCE SUMMARY

Army Form C. 2118.

Vol 6

Place	Date	Hour	Summary of Events and Information	Remarks and references to Appendices
RENINGHELST	1916 NOVEMBER 1st		Inspection of the 123rd Infantry Brigade by G.O.C. 2nd Army. Expehun.	Operation Order 1A
	2nd		C.F. Dingwall assumed command of the company. Relieved 122nd M.G. company in ST ELOI sector.	
VOORMEZEELE	3rd		Trench troops. Inspection of line and gun-positions by G.O.C. 1st Division.	
	4th & 5 & 6 & 7		Trench troops. Wire cutting by artillery, co-operation by M.G. Company. Trench troops. During the six days tour of the trenches machine gun indirect fire was brought to bear on specified targets behind the enemy front line, i.e. Cross Roads, Farms, and communication trenches.	
	8th		Relieved by 122nd M.G. Coy. Returned to Rest Billets, Chippewa Camp.	"N° I
CHIPPEWA CAMP	9.10.11.		Rest Billets.	
	12th		G.O.C. 123rd Infantry Brigade presented Distribution of medal ribbons Sgt Havercigs, Cpl Saunders and Pte Hall.	
	13th		Inspection by G.O.C. 123rd Infantry Brigade.	
	14th		Rest Billets. Officers reconnoitre line ST ELOI sector. Fatigue party of 2 100 men to lay trench railway at Dickebusch.	
VOORMEZEELE	15th 16-21		Relieved 122nd M.G. Company ST ELOI sector. Trench troops. On 21st bombardment by Artillery, co-operation by M.G. company. During the six days tour of the trenches machine gun indirect fire was brought to bear on specified points behind the enemy front line i.e Cross Roads, Farms and communication trenches	"N° II

WAR DIARY or INTELLIGENCE SUMMARY

Army Form C. 2118.

Place	Date	Hour	Summary of Events and Information	Remarks and references to Appendices
	NOVEMBER 1916			
VOORMEZEELE	22nd		Relieved by 122nd M.G. company. Returned to Reat Billets, QUEBEC CAMP. R.E. Nº 9 F.E.L.S.E. One officer and 16 men with 8 guns took up defensive positions in G.H.Q. reserve line	Operation Order Nº VIII
QUEBEC CAMP	23rd–24th		Reat-Billets. On 23rd Fatigue party of 1 officer and 50 men reported to R.E. Nº BEELE.	
	24th		In lieu company relief of G.H.Q reserve line	11 Nº IV
	27		Relieved 122nd M.G. Coy in St ELOI section. 2/Lt F.L. Shaw proceeded to A.M.G. course	" Nº V
VOORMEZEELE	28–30th		at CAMIERS. French troops	
			General	
			Rain and frosty weather experienced throughout the month. The general health of the company was good. No cases of trench foot have occured so far in the company. 6 men attended courses i.e. MG Course CAMIERS, signalling course Zuytpeene, R.E. instruction 233 Field company. Drivers Bodle and Batten of the transport section were badly injured owing to which mount slipping on the wet forward roads. 2 officers C.S.M. Barnes & 3 other ranks went on leave during the month. 2/Lt Harvey joined the company from the Base 18/11/1916. Lt Oberly rejoined the company from 56 M.G. Company on the 19/11/1916. The company has retired a canteen the profits forming a company fund.	

C.F. Dinwell CAPTAIN.
COMDG. 123RD COY. MACHINE GUN CORPS.

~~Secret~~

Operation Order No I by
Captain C. F. Dingwall
Commanding 123rd Machine gun company.

I. The 123rd M.G. Coy will relieve the 122nd M.G. Coy. in the St ELoi Sector on Thursday 2nd NOVEMBER

II. The 123rd M.G. Coy. will be at VOORMEZEELE at 10.30AM on the 2nd NOVEMBER.

III. One guide per gun will meet the relieving company at M.G. Coy. H.Q. VOORMEZEELE and will conduct the relieving teams to their positions in the trenches

IV. Officers will take up the following positions:- ~~Lt Reid~~ Defence line; Lt Thomas. Bus House etc, 2Lt Webster. Right section; 2Lt Shaw. Spoil Bank. Lt Hanson.

V. All tripods and ten filled belt boxes per gun will be taken over, all R.E. stores, & trench stores will be checked and duplicate list sent to C.H.Q.

VI. The Transport Officers will arrange to take all guns, spare parts etc up to the trenches on the 1st inst. A guard detailed elsewhere will accompany same.

VII. Officers and N.C.Os. are responsible that men do not wander about VOORMEZEELE or the trenches during the relief

VIII. All Huts, cook-houses, latrines etc to be left scrupulously clean.

IX * Code word for completion of relief. "SUREZKING". Acknowledge.

Details No 1 War Diary & file
2. T.O.
3 No 1 Sect. Officer
4 2 " "
5 3 " "
6 4 " "
7 123 Infantry Brigade
8 122 M.G. Coy.

Scott LT. & ADJT.
123RD COY. MACHINE GUN CORPS.

Secret:

- Operation Orders No I by
Capt C.F. Dingwall commanding
123rd Machine Gun Coy

I. The 123rd M.G. Coy will be relieved by 122nd M.G. Coy on Wednesday Nov 8. 16. in the St Eloi section

II. The relieving company is expected to be at Coy H.Q. at VOORMEZEELE at 11 am on the 8th Nov.

III. Section officers will detail one guide per gun, to report to C.H.Q. at 10.30 am.

IV. Guides will conduct relieving teams to gun positions & Billets.
Section Officers will conduct relieving officers over all gun positions & Billets.

V. All tripods & ten filled belt Boxes per gun will be handed over.
All R.E. stores, trench stores & bulk ammunition will be handed over.
Duplicate receipts of all stores handed over will be handed in to C.H.Q. on completion of relief.

VI. All guns, spare part boxes, etc, diaries, officers kits etc. will be dumped at Coy H.Q. and will remain under a guard of 1 N.C.O. & 3 men, detailed elsewhere, until taken away by company transport on the night of 8th Nov.

VII. Section Officers will render a summary of work done, work to be done, and trench stores, to be handed over, by 9.0 am tomorrow

Secret

Operation Orders II by
Capt. G. Dingwall
commanding 173rd M.G. Coy.

I. The 173rd M.G. Coy will relieve the 122nd M.G. Coy in the ST. ELOI sector on Wednesday the 15th Nov 16.

II. The 173rd M.G. Coy. will be at VOORMEZEELE at 10.30 am on the 15th Nov.

III. One guide per gun will meet the relieving company at M.G. Coy H.Q. VOORMEZEELE. & will conduct the relieving teams to their positions in the trenches.

IV. Officers will take up the positions in the trenches which are detailed elsewhere.

V. All tripods and ten filled belt boxes per gun will be taken over.
All R.E. stores, & trench stores will be taken over.

VI. Officers must check everything taken over & hand in a signed duplicate copy of the list to C. H. Q.

VII. The relief will be carried out as expeditiously as possible; gun teams will keep together and officers & N.C.O's will see to it that individual gunners do not wander about the VILLAGE & trenches whilst the relief is being carried out.

VIII. All section officers will report to Coy H.Q. on completion of relief.

IX. On completion of relief wire "MORE OVER"

X. Acknowledge.

(signed)
A. McKie Reid
173rd M.G. Coy

In the Field
14.11.16.

VIII. Tomorrow, breakfast ration only will be provided; and a hot meal will be ready for the company on arrival at Transport Lines.

IX. Section Officers will be responsible that these orders are strictly adhered to.

X. The code word for completion of relief will be "Acetylene".

XI. Acknowledge.

In the Field
4.30 pm
Nov 19th 1916.

(signed) A. McKie Reid
2/Lt
for OC. 183rd M.G.Coy.

No 1. War Diary
2. OC I Section
3. OC II "
4. OC III "
5. OC IV "
6. T.O. 183 M.G.C
7. 183 Infty Brigade
8. 122 M.G.C.

SECRET.

Copy No: ....

Operation Orders. No. 3. by CAPTAIN C.F. DINGWALL commanding 123rd Machine Gun Company.

I. The 123rd M.G.Coy. will be relieved by the 122nd M.G.Coy. in the ST. ELOI sector on the 22nd inst.

II. One guide from each gun team will be at C.H.Q. at 10.30 A.M. on the 22nd inst.

III. Section officers will send down a copy of French Stores to be handed over by 8 A.M. on 22nd inst.

IV. Lieut. HANSON will take two guns to RUINS DUMP. The guns are to remain there under two men until transport arrives in evening. Transport officer will make arrangement for this.

V. Lieut. HANSON will also take two guns & spare parts boxes complete to Eastern entrance of ECLUSE TR. at a point about I.32.a.60.60. These guns will remain there under a guard of two men till taken away by men under 2/Lieut. HARVEY. The guard of two men will then return to H.Q.

VI. Lieut. THOMAS will detail 1 Cpl. 2 L/Cpls. & 13 ptes. to go into RESERVE LINE with 2/Lieut HARVEY. Detailed orders will be issued to these two officers.

VII. On completion of relief Sections will move back under Section officers to QUEBEC CAMP.

VIII. The Second-in-command will arrange with O.C. 122nd M.G.Coy. to take over all huts, tents etc. at present occupied by 122nd M.G.Coy. He will also arrange with Transport officer to take all necessary stores to QUEBEC CAMP.

IX. Full rations will be issued on night of 21st inst.

X. Officers and NCO's are responsible that men do not wander aimlessly about the VILLAGE & trenches during relief & do not straggle on the way back.

XI. All billets, emplacements, latrines etc will be left scrupulously clean.

XII. Remaining guns for RESERVE LINE will be found as follows:- 4 guns from No.1. Sec? 2 guns from No.2. Sec?

XIII. On completion of relief wire — "FEED-BLOCK".

XIV. Acknowledge.

In the field.
10 A.M.
NOV. 21. 1916.

A. McRae Reid.
2/LT. & ADJT.
123RD COY. MACHINE GUN CORPS.

No 1. War Diary & File
- 2. Second-in-command & T.O.
- 3. No.1. Sec. Officer
- 4. No. 2   "
- 5. No. 3   "
- 6. No. 4   "
- 7. 123rd Inf. Brig.
- 8. 122nd M.G.Coy.
- 9.

Secret

Operation Orders 4. by
Capt C.F. Dingwall
commanding 103rd M.G. Coy.

I. The garrison holding the G.H.Q No 2 line will be relieved tomorrow 25th Nov 1916.

II. 1 corporal, 2 lance-corporals, 13 men under Lt HANSON will take over the on-guard in the line. The men are detailed elsewhere.

III. One guide from each gun will be at SCOTTISH Wood at 10 am. tomorrow.

IV. The officer taking over will sign for all guns, stores etc. taken over.
Each officer will retain a copy & a copy will be handed in to C.H.Q. after relief.

V. Relief will be reported complete by the officer who is relieved.

(signed) A McKie-Reid
2nd Lt & adjt
103rd M.G. Coy

24-11-16

Secret   Copy No. 1

Operation Orders No. 5 by
Capt. D. D. Dingwall
Commanding 123rd Machine Gun Coy.

I. The 123rd Machine Gun Coy will relieve the 122nd M.G. Coy in the "St Eloi" section on Monday 27th November 1916.

II. The 123rd M.G. Coy will be at VOORMEZEELE at 10.30 am on the 27th Nov.

III. One guide per gun will meet the relieving company at M.G. Coy H.Q. VOORMEZEELE will conduct the relieving teams to their position in the trenches.

IV. Teams will take up the following positions in the trenches:-
2/Lt Homan Spoil Bank, 2/Lt Harvey, Bus House, & 2/Lt Webster on the right or Lt Hanson DEFENCE LINE

V. All tripods and ten filled belt boxes per gun will be taken over, all R.E. stores & trench stores will be taken over, and checked, and duplicate list sent to C.M.Q.

VI. The T.O. will have 2 limbers at C.H.Q. QUEBEC Camp at 3pm 26th inst to take guns, spare parts Boxes etc, up to the trenches. A guard detailed elsewhere will accompany same.

VII. On the 27th he will arrange to have limbers at C.H.Q. QUEBEC CAMP at 9.30 am to take spare kit blankets & Coy stores etc to the stores.

VIII Sp Maercen will send the reserve team to H.Q. at 10 am with one man after leaving the guns at H.Q. they will remain there, and act as escort to the section of the reserve on its going into the reserve lines. On completion of reserve relief, both men from each team will report at H.Q. on relieving at position in VOORMEZEELE DEFENCE LINE.

IX All tests in camp, with exception of the breakfast ration will be issued to each man before 5am on the 27th.

X Officers T.N.C.O's are responsible that men do not wander about VOORMEZEELE and the breaches during relief.

XI All tents, huts, cook-house, latrines to be kept scrupulously clean.

XII Code word for completion of relief "VERMOUTH"

Acknowledge.

Inthefield   Stanley Scott 2/Lt Inf
Nov 26 1916.   123 M.G. Coy
Detail.
No 1 This ready to file
   2   T.O.
   3   No 1. Section Officer
   4   2   "   "
   5   3   "   "
   6   4   "   "
   7   123 Infty Brigade
   8   122nd M.G. Coy.

123rd Infantry Brigade.

SUMMARY OF CASUALTIES DURING MONTH OF NOVEMBER, 1916.

Regiment.	Rank.	Name.	Killed. Wounded.	Remarks.
11th Queen's	2/Lieut.	TUGWELL, F.W.	Wounded.	
do.	do.	TODD, H.M.	Wounded.	
do.	do.	O'BYRNE, D.C.H.	Wounded.	(Slightly, at duty.)

OTHER RANKS.

do.   KILLED - 5,   WOUNDED 19 (incl. one slightly, at duty)

10th R.W.Kents,	2/Lieut.	POCOCK, E.M.	Wounded.	

OTHER RANKS.

do.   KILLED - 2,   WOUNDED - 8, (incl. three Shell Shock)

23rd Middlesex,	2/Lieut.	BARCLAY, H.L.	Wounded.	

OTHER RANKS.

do.   KILLED - 1,   WOUNDED 2   (incl. one slightly, at duty)

20th Durham
  Light Infy.   OTHER RANKS.

          KILLED - 2,   WOUNDED - 12   (Killed includes one
                                          accidental)
                                        (Wounded include 6
                                          slightly, at duty)

WAR DIARY
or
INTELLIGENCE SUMMARY
(Erase heading not required.)

Army Form C. 2118

Instructions regarding War Diaries and Intelligence Summaries are contained in F.S. Regs., Part II. and the Staff Manual respectively. Title Pages will be prepared in manuscript.

Place	Date	Hour	Summary of Events and Information	Remarks and references to Appendices
	Decr			
Voormezeele	1		Trench troops in St Eloi Sector.	
	2		Relieved by 122nd M.G. Coy. Returned to rest billets at QUEBEC CAMP.	O.O. 6
Quebec Camp	3 &4		In rest billets	
Reninghelst	5		Inter- company relief of garrison in Reserve Line	
			Inspection of Transport by O.C. 41st Div: Train	O.O. 7
	6 &7		Rest Billets - men practised in revolver shooting.	
	8		Relieved 122nd M.G. Coy in the St Eloi Sector.	O.O. 8
Voormezeele	9 &10		Trench troops.	
	11		Capt C.F. Dingwall went on leave to U.K. Lt Scott assumed command of the Company.	
	12		12 men attached to 1st Canadian Tunnelling Company.	O.O. 9
	13			
	14		Relieved by 122nd M.G. Coy. Returned to rest billets at QUEBEC CAMP	
Reninghelst	15 &16		In rest billets	
	17		Inter Company relief of G.H.Q. R line	O.O. 10
	18	am		
	19	9.15	Inspection of transport by G.O.C. 41st Division at Micmac Camp	
	20		Inspection of Brigade by G.O.C. 123rd Infy Bde, as rehearsal for	
	21		Inspection of Brigade by C. in C who left a message of praise & cheer to the whole Brigade.	
			Company had hot meal at Transport Lines, and then carried out relief of 122nd M.G. Coy in the St Eloi Sector.	O.O. 11
Voormezeele	22		Trench troops.	
	23	am	Capt Dingwall arrived back from leave and reassumed command of the Company.	
	25	8. 7	Enemy blew camouflet opposite the left sub-sector, but no damage to our Line or Works resulted.	
	26		The Transport Officer Lt. R.M Doherty proceeded on leave to U.K. Lt Scott took over work of Transport Officer.	
	27	8-8.25 pm	Intensive Indirect Fire shoot in cooperation with Medium and Light trench mortars.	
	28		Relieved by 122nd M.G. Coy	O.O. 12

Army Form C. 2118.

WAR DIARY
or
INTELLIGENCE SUMMARY

(Erase heading not required.)

Instructions regarding War Diaries and Intelligence Summaries are contained in F. S. Regs., Part II. and the Staff Manual respectively. Title Pages will be prepared in manuscript.

Place	Date	Hour	Summary of Events and Information	Remarks and references to Appendices
Reninghelst	Dec 29 30		In rest billets - gun cleaning, kit inspection, issuing of clothing etc Christmas dinner was given to Company, as on 25th they were in trench troops. The G.O.C. 123rd Infantry Brigade visited the Company during the dinner, and drank the health of the Company, upon which, 3 hearty cheers were given to him. Church Parades and bathing parades in morning, half holiday in afternoon.	
	31		Inter Company relief of garrison in G.H.Q. R. Line.	O.O. 13
			During the month, while in the line, indirect fire was carried out throughout all the hours of darkness, and during the daytime in foggy weather, on enemy dumps, trench tramways, billets and reserve and communication trenches. During the month, 2 Officers and 5 O.R. proceeded on leave to U.K. There has been much rain during the month, and on two occasions snow fell necessitating great care to prevent tracks being made to emplacements etc.	

A. Nicols
Lt. & Adjt.
123RD COY. MACHINE GUN CORPS.

From O.C.123rd.M.G.Coy.

To H.Q.123rd.Inf.Brig.

Attached please find WAR- DIARY for this

unit for the month of DECEMBER.1916.

DEC.31st 1916.

A. M. Giles
Lieut.and Adjt.
123rd M.G.Coy.

Secret   Copies   War Diary

Operation Orders No.6 by Captain
C.F. Dingwall, commanding 123rd M. G. Coy.

---

1. The 123rd M. G. Coy will be relieved by the 122nd M G Coy in the ST ELOI sector on the second instant.

2. One guide per gun team will be at C. H. Q at 10.30 am on the 2nd instant.

3. Section Officers will send in a copy of trench stores to be haded over, by 8 am on the 2nd instant.

4. Lt Thomas will send two guns to Ruins dump with a guard of 2 men, until taken away by the Transport. The other 2 guns of the section will be taken to the Eastern end of Ecluse trench and relieve 122ng M. G. Coy in the left sector of GH.Q reserve line. 1 L/cpl and 3 men will be detailed by Lt Thomas to man these two guns, the men to belong to the teams that the guns belong to. O.C. 2 section will detail 1 L/cpl and 3 men and 2 guns for G.H.Q. R line. O.C. 3 section will detail 1 Cpl and 3 men and 2 guns from teams 9 and 10 for G.H.Q. R line. O.C. 2 section will detail 4 men and 2 guns of the same teams.

5. Lt Thomas will be I/c of the G.H.Q. R line, and will take up his position there on completion of his section relief. He will take over and check tripods, ammunition, R.E. and trench stores, handed over by 122nd M. G. Coy in that line. The N.C.O's and men detailed for the reserve line will report to C.S.M. as soon as their teams arrive at C.H.Q, with the exception of men who are detailed from No.1 section, who relieve 122nd M. G. Coy under arrangement of Lt Thomas.

6. On completion of relief, sections will move back under section officers to QUEBEC CAMP.

(continued)

7. The C.Q.M.S. will take over all huts, tents etc occupied by 122nd M.G. Coy. He will also arrange with the T.O. to take all necessary stores etc to QUEBEC CAMP on the 2nd instant, also water cart.

8. The Transport Officer will arrange to have the half limber to Ruins dump and limbers to HQ. to take guns etc to QUEBEC CAMP on the 2nd instant.

9. Full rations will be issued on the 1st instant.

10. Officers and N.C.O's are responsible that men do not wander about VOORMEZEELE and the trenches during relief, or straggle on the road to camp.

11. All billets, emplacements, latrines etc will be left scrupulously clean.

12. On completion of relief, wire "SURETHING" "acknowledge".

(signed) S. Scott
Lt & Adjt
123 M.G. Company.

In the Field
1.12.1916.

Secret   Copy __WAR DIARY__

Operation Order No.7 by Captain C.F. Dingwall, commanding 123 M. G. Company.
---

1. The garrison holding the G.H.Q reserve line will be relieved tomorrow, 5th December 1916.

2. 1 Cpl, 2 L/cpls and 13 men under 2/Lt Webster will take over the Machine guns in this line. N.C.O's and men detailed elsewhere.

3. Guides detailed by Lt. Thomas will be at Scottish Wood at 10 am tomorrow to guide the relief to the gun positions.

4. The Transport Officer will arrange to have a half limber at the Duck-walk at 9 am. The limber will wait for the relieved party.

5. The relieving Officer will sign for all guns, stores etc taken over, and a copy will be sent to C.H.Q.

6. Iron Rations, Field dressings, gas helmets and steel helmets of the men detailed for G.H.Q. reserve line will be inspected by 2/Lt Webster before leaving QUEBEC CAMP.

7. The relief will be reported omplete by Lt. Thomas on returning to Camp.

(Signed) Scott

Lt and Adjt, 123 Machine Gun Coy.

In the Field,
 4th Decr 1916.

Detail 1   War diary & File
        2   "   "   Duplicate
        3   Lt Thomas
        4   2/Lt Webster
        5   Transport Officer
        6   123rd Infy Bde.

Secret   Copy

Operation Order 8 by Captain C.F. Dingwall
Commanding 123rd Machine Gun Company.

1. The 123rd M.G. Coy will relieve the 122nd M.G. Coy in the St Eloi sector, on Friday 8/12/1916.

2. The 123rd M.G. Coy will be at VOORMEZEELE at 10-30 am on the 8th instant.

3. One guide per gun team will meet the 122nd M.G. Coy at M.G. Coy H.Q. at VOORMEZEELE and will conduct the relieving teams to their positions in the trenches.

4. Officers will take up the following positions:-
   Lt Hanson, Spoil Bank., 2/Lt Harvey, Bus House etc., Lt Thomas, Right Section, 2/Lt Webster, Voormezeele defence line.

5. All tripods and ten filled belt boxes per gun will be taken over. All R.E. stores and trench stores will be checked and duplicate list sent to C.H.Q.

6. The T.O. will have two limbers at duck-walk, Bde H.Q. at 3 pm on the 7th instant, to take guns, spare parts boxes etc up to the trenches. A guard, detailed elsewhere will accompany same.

7. On the 8th instant he will arrange to have limbers at duck-walk, Bde H.Q. at 9-30 am, to take spare kit, blankets and Coy stores etc to the stores.

8. 2/Lt Webster will arrange to have guns, spare parts boxes etc, in reserve line, sent to C.H.Q, VOORMEZEELE by 10 am. One man from each gun position will remain and act as guide to 122 M.G. Coy. On completion of the reserve line relief, all men will report to C.H.Q.

9. Full rations, with the exception of the breakfast ration, will be issued to each man before 7 am on the 8th instant.

10. Officers and N.C.O's are responsible that men do not wander about VOORMEZEELE and the trenches during relief.

11. All tents, huts, cookhouses, latrines to be left scrupulously clean.

12. Code word for completion of relief "EMPIRE".

13. Acknowledge.

                                      (sd)   S. Scott
                              Lt & Adjt, 123rd Machine Gun Coy.

In the Field,
   6/12/1916.

Detail 1   War Diary & File
        2   "   Duplicate
        3   Transport Officer
        4   No.1 Section Officer
        5   No.2 Section Officer
        6   No.3 Section Officer
        7   No.4 Section Officer
        8   122 M.G. Company
        9   123 Infy Brigade
       10   Corps M.G. Officer
       11   122 Infy Brigade.

Secret   COPY. 1.

Operation Orders 9 by Lieut. S. Scott,
commanding 123rd Machine Gun Company.
----

1. The 123rd M. G. Coy will be relieved by the 122nd M.G. Coy
   in the St Eloi Sector on December 14th, 1916.

2. The relieving Company is expected to be at VOORMEZEELE at
   10.30 am.

3. One guide per gun team will report at C.H.Q. at 10 am.

4. Section Officers will send in a list of stores to be
   handed over, before 9 am on December 14th to H.Q.

5. Lt Hanson will send 2 guns to "RUINS DUMP with a guard of
   2 men, until taken away by the transport in the evening.
   The other 2 guns of No.4 Section will relieve the 2
   extreme left guns of C.H.Q. R Line. A L/c and 7 men will
   man these 2 guns.
   O.C. No.1 Section will detail 1 Cpl and 7 men and to take 2
   guns.
   O.C. No.2 Section will detail 4 men to take 2 guns.
   O.C. No.3 Section will detail 1 L/c and 7 men to take
   2 guns to garrison reserve line.
   The N.C.Os and men detailed to garrison the reserve line
   will report to C.H.Q. on completion of their Sections relief,
   with the exception of the N.C.O and men detailed from No.4
   Section. Officers commanding Sections will send in to
   C.H.Q before 8 am on the 14th the names of the N.C.Os and men
   so detailed.

6. The same guns and spare parts boxes, which were in the
   Reserve Line last term, will not be placed there during the
   forthcoming term. This, in order that spare parts boxes etc
   may be checked and replenished during the rest period.

7. Lt Hanson will be i/c C.H.Q. R Line and will take up his
   position there on completion of his Section relief. He will
   take over and check all stores, tripods, ammunition etc
   handed over by 122nd M.G. Coy in that line, and will send a
   list of such stores etc to C.H.Q.

8. On completion of relief, Sections will move back to QUEBEC
   CAMP under Section Officers. Transport for packs, and
   Officers' chargers will be provided at DICKEBUSCH - detail
   elsewhere.

9. The C.Q.M.S. will take over all huts, tents etc at present
   occupied by 122nd M.G. Coy. He will also arrange with T.O.
   to have all necessary stores and the water cart taken to
   QUEBEC CAMP on the 14th instant.

10. Rations, with the exception of the dinner ration will be
    issued on the 13th. The C.Q.M.S. will arrange to have the
    dinner rations at QUEBEC CAMP on the morning on the 14th.
    The Company cooks will then proceed to prepare a hot meal for
    the Company on its arrival on completion of relief. For this
    purpose the Company cooks will be sent to QUEBEC CAMP
    immediately after breakfast on the 14th.

11. The T.O. will arrange to have a half limber sent to RUINS
    DUMP at dusk on the 14th, and sufficient transport at C.H.Q.
    to take guns etc to QUEBEC CAMP.

12. Officers and N.C.Os are responsible that men do not wander
    about VOORMEZEELE and the trenches during relief, and do
    not straggle on the way to Camp.

Operation Orders 9 (continued)

13 All billets, emplacements, latrines etc must be left scrupulously clean.

14 On completion of relief, wire "LEAVE". ~~Acknowledge~~.

15 Acknowledge.

         (sd) A.McKie Reid, Lt & Adjt
         123rd Machine Gun Company.

In the Field,
 Decr 14th 1916.

To.
1. War Diary
2. Duplicate
3. O.C. No.1 Section
4. " 2 "
5. " 3 "
6. " 4 "
7. Transport Officer
8. Xth Corps M.G.O.
9. 123rd Infantry Brigade
10. 122nd Machine Gun Coy
11. 122nd Infantry Brigade.

Secret

Operation Order 10 by Lt. S. Scott
commdg 123rd Machine Gun Company.

1. The Garrison holding the G.H.Q. R. line will be relieved tomorrow the 17th instant.

2. One Cpl, 2 L/Cpls and 13 men under 2/Lt Shaw will take over this line.

3. Guides detailed by Lt Hanson will be at Scottish Wood at 10 am tomorrow to guide the relief to the gun positions.

4. The T.O. will arrange to have a half limber at the Duck-walk at 9 am to carry mens' packs etc. This limber will wait at Scottish Wood for the outcoming party.

5. The relieving officer will sign for all guns, stores etc taken over. A list will be sent to H.Q.

6. Iron Rations, Field dressings, gas helmets and steel helmets will be examined by 2/Lt Shaw before the men detailed, leave this Camp.

7. The relief will be reported complete by Lt Hanson on his return to Quebec Camp.

8. The unexpired portion of the day's ration will be taken.

9. One blanket per man will be taken and the other blanket handed into the Section Sergeant to be placed with the Sections blankets.

10. Acknowledge.

(sd) A.McKie Reid, Lt & Adjt

123rd Machine Gun Company.

Decr 16th 1916.

Detail 1 War Diary & File
        2 Duplicate
        3 Lt Hanson
        4 2/Lt Shaw
        5 Transport Officer
        6 H.Q. 123rd Infy Brigade.

Secret

Operation Orders 11 by Adjut S. Scott,
commanding 123rd Machine Gun Company.

1. The 123rd M.G. Coy will relieve the 122nd M.G. Coy in the St Eloi Sector, on the 21st Decr 1916.

2. The 123rd M.G. Coy will be at Voormezeele at   on Thursday, when guides to the gun positions will be provided by 122nd M.G. Coy to meet the 123rd M.G. Coy.

3. Officers will take up the following positions in the trenches:-
    2/Lt Harvey   - Right Sector
    2/Lt Shaw   - Voormezeele
    2/Lt Webster - Bus House Group
    Lt Hanson   - Spoil Bank Group.

4. All tripods, ten filled belt boxes per gun, all trench stores and R.E. stores, will be taken over and checked. A signed list of the foregoing will be sent to C.H.Q.

5. The Transport Officer will have one limber at the duck-walk Bde H.Q. at 1.30 pm on Wednesday to take the guns up to Voormezeele. A guard of 1 N.C.O. and 3 men detailed elsewhere, will accompany this limber. The guard will take the unexpended portion of Wednesday's rations, and rations for Thursday, with them.

6. On the 21st the T.O. will arrange to have limbers at duck-walk at   to take spare kit, blankets and Company stores to Q.M. stores.

7. 2/Lt Shaw will arrange to have guns, spare parts boxes etc sent to H.Q. Voormezeele by 12 noon. One man from each gun position will remain as guides for 122nd M.G. Coy in the Reserve Line. On completion of the R line relief, all men will report to C.H.Q.

8. Full rations, with the exception of the breakfast rations, will be issued to each man before 7 am on the 21st.

9. Officers and N.C.O.s are responsible that men do not wander aimlessly about the trenches and roads during relief.

10. All tents, huts, cookhouses, latrines etc in QUEBEC CAMP must be left scrupulously clean.

11. On completion of relief, wire "Leicester".

12. Acknowledge.

(sd) A.Maris Reid, Lt & Adjt

123rd Machine Gun Company

In the Field
   Decr 20th 1916.

To.
    1   War Diary and File
    2   Duplicate
    3   O.C. Section 1
    4   "   2
    5   "   3
    6   "   4
    7   Transport Officer
    8   Xth Corps M.G.O.
    9   123rd Infy Bde
   10   122nd M.G. Coy
   11   122nd Infy Bde.

Secret

War Diary

Operation Order 12 by Captain C.F. Dingwall commanding 123rd Machine Gun Company.

1. The 123rd M.G. Coy will be relieved by the 122nd M.G. Coy in the St Eloi Sector on Dec 28th 1916.

2. The relieving Company is expected to be at VOORMEZEELE at 10.30 am. One guide per gun team will report at H.Q. at 10 am to conduct the relieving teams.

3. Section Officers will send in statement of work done and list of trench stores to be handed over, by 8 am on the 28th inst.

4. O.C. No.4 Section will send 4 guns to "RUINS DUMP" with a guard of 2 men to wait until guns are taken away by transport at dusk. The guns of No.3 Section will be sent down to Rest Billets on relief.

5. O.C. No.1 Section will detail 1 L/C and 3 men and 1 runner
   " " 2 " " " 4 men
   " " 3 " " " 1 L/c and 3 men
   " " 4 " " " Cpl Wilson and 3 men.
   to relieve the garrison of G.H.Q. R Line. The guns of Nos.1 and 2 Sections will be taken.
   Officers will send in names of men detailed by 8 am on the 28th inst.
   Lt Thomas will be in command of the R Line garrison, and will take over all stores, tripods etc and give receipt to 122nd M.G. Coy.

6. On completion of relief, Sections will move back under Section Officers to QUEBEC CAMP.

7. The C.Q.M.S. will make arrangements with the T.O. to have all necessary stores taken over to QUEBEC CAMP, and will have a hot meal prepared for the Company on its arrival.
   The Company cooks, and one man per Section, will parade at H.Q. at 8 am. Section Officers will detail these men.

8. Section Officers and N.C.Os are responsible that men do not wander aimlessly about the trenches and village during relief, and that they do straggle on the way to Camp.

9. All billets, emplacements, latrines etc will be left scrupulously clean. Pte HAMBER R.A.M.C. will visit each billet, emplacement and latrine in the Sector, before relief, and report on their cleanliness to the Adjutant.

10. Separate orders are issued to T.O. and a copy to each Section Officer.

11. On completion of relief, wire "LOUNGE".

12. Acknowledge.

                                              (sd) A. McKie Reid, Lt & Adjt
                                                123rd Machine Gun Company.

In the Field
   December 27th 1916.

To.

1	War Diary			
2	Duplicate			
3	O.C. No.1 Section			
4	" " 2 "			
5	" " 3 "			
6	" " 4 "		10.	123rd Infantry Brigade
7	Transport Officer		11.	122nd " "
8	Xth Corps M.G.O.			
9	122nd M.G. Company			

<u>Secret</u>

Operation Orders 13 by Captain C.F. Dingwall
commanding 123rd Machine Gun Company.
_____

1. The garrison in the G.H.Q. reserve Line will be relieved tomorrow, December 31st.

2. 1 Cpl., 2 L/cpls., and 13 men under 2/Lt Harvey will take over the line. These men are detailed elsewhere.

3. Guides, detailed by 2/Lt Webster will be at Scottish Wood at 10.30 am tomorrow, to guide the relief to the gun positions.

4. The T.O. will arrange to have a half limber at the Duckwalk at 9 am to carry packs. This limber will wait at Scottish Wood for the outcoming party.

5. The relieving Officer will sign for all guns, stores etc taken over. A list will be sent to H.Q.

6. Iron rations, field dressings, gas helmets and steel helmets will be inspected by 2/Lt Harvey before the relieving party leave this Camp.

7. The relief will be reported complete by 2/Lt Webster on his return to Camp.

8. The unexpended portion of the day's ration will be taken.

9. One blanket per man will be taken, and the other blanket handed to the Section Sgt to be placed with the Sections' blankets.

10. Acknowledge.

                                           (sd) A.McKie Reid, Lt & Ajt

                                           123rd Machine Gun Company.

In the Field,
    December 30th 1916.

1. War Diary
2. Duplicate
3. 2/Lt Webster
4. 2/Lt Harvey
5. Transport Officer
6. H.Q. 123rd Infy: Bde:

WAR DIARY or INTELLIGENCE SUMMARY

(Erase heading not required.)

Army Form C. 2118.

123 M G Coy   Vol 8

Place	Date 1917.	Hour	Summary of Events and Information	Remarks and references to Appendices
Reninghelst	1		Bathing parade. Preparing guns etc for Line.	
Voormezeele	2		Relieved 122nd M.G. Coy in St Eloi Sector.	O.O.14
	3&4		"	
	5		Long range shoot (indirect fire). Cpl Edden proceeded on course of anti aircraft instruction.	
Reninghelst	6		"	
	7		Relieved by 122nd M.G. Coy in St Eloi Sector.	O.O.15
	8&9		Rest billets, gun cleaning, route march etc. Inspection of guns by Ordnance armourer, who pronounced them both very serviceable and well cared for. Army Commander came round all camps in the Brigade.	
	10		Inter Company relief of G.H.Q. 2nd Line.	O.O.16
	11&12		U.S.M. Wardle left to take up a permanent commission in the 8th Bett: Northumberland Fusiliers.	
	13		Tactical exercise, gun drill, stoppages, stripping etc.	
Voormezeele	14		Relieved 122nd M.G. Coy in St Eloi Sector.	O.O.17
	15		Pte Wickens proceeded on M.G. course at Camiers.	
	16		Trench troops.	
	17		" Sgt. Barton & Cpl Woulidge arrived as reinforcements.	
	18		Co-operation in raid by 11th Queens., 12 guns, 10 indirect fire, and one on either flank giving covering fire. One prisoner taken. Company fired 25,000 rounds in 15 minutes. Cpl George proceeded on course of anti-aircraft instruction.	
	19		Trench troops.	
	20		C.Q.M.S. Scottorn proceeded to U.K. as a candidate for a commission. L/Sgt Philip appointed A/C.Q.M.S., Sgt Horridge appointed A/C.S.M.	
Reninghelst	21		Relieved by 122nd M.G. Coy in St Eloi Sector. During tour 35 men attached to R.E. to build concrete dugouts etc.	O.O.18
	22		Rest billets. Instruction of 20 men attached from Infantry.	
	24		Inter Company relief of G.H.Q. 2nd Line.	O.O.19
	25		Bathing parade.	
	26		Tactical exercises carried out. Guns inspected by Ordnance armourer. Usual drill carried out.	
Voormezeele	27		Relieved 122nd M.G. Coy in St Eloi Sector.	O.O.20
	28.29 30&31		Trench troops.	

Army Form C. 2118.

WAR DIARY
or
INTELLIGENCE SUMMARY
(Erase heading not required.)

Place	Date 1917	Hour	Summary of Events and Information	Remarks and references to Appendices
			General A large amount of indirect fire was carried out during the month, the Company gradually increasing the total to 10,000 rounds a night. The fire was carried out every night and during foggy weather, was on enemy dumps, dugouts, roads etc, throughout the month during tours in trenches. The Company seemed to have got completely the upper hand of enemy machine guns in the St Eloi Sector. There were no cases of trench feet during the month. One shell burst in Headquarters, killing a servant and wounding the artificer, signalling corporal, and pioneer. Great many promotions took place on January 24th to complete the establishment. It might be added that, every round expended by this Company, the empty case is returned to the Base. Lt A. McKie Reid was evacuated sick on the 29th. Intense cold experienced during the month. Health of the Company - good. During the month 2 O.R. killed and 3 wounded. Lt Thomas proceeded on sick leave to Boulogne for dental purposes. 3 O.R. proceeded on leave to U.K. C.P.Dirwell Captain. Commdg: 123rd Coy: Machine Gun Corps.	

Secret

Operation Orders No.14 by Captain C.F.Dingwall
commanding 123rd Machine Gun Company.

1. The 123rd M. G. Coy will relieve the 122nd M. G. Coy in the St Eloi Sector on January 2nd 1917.

2. Guides from 122nd M.G. Coy will be at Voormezeele at 10.30am to conduct the relieving gun teams to their respective gun positions.

3. Section Officers and their Sections will take up the following positions in the Line:-
   - Lt. Thomas   VOORMEZEELE DEFENCES
   - 2/Lt Shaw   BUS HOUSE GROUP
   - 2/Lt Webster   RIGHT GROUP
   - Lt Hanson   SPOIL BANK GROUP.
   - 2/Lt Harvey will be attached to 2/Lt Webster for duty.

4. All tripods, 10 filled belt boxes per gun, all trench stores and R.E. stores will be taken over, checked; and signed for by the relieving Section Officers. A signed list will be handed in to C.H.Q.

5. The Transport Officer will arrange to have one limber at Duck-walk on the evening of the 1st inst at time arranged to take the 8 guns up to Voormezeele. One sergeant and 3 men will be detailed elsewhere, as a guard, to accompany the guns. The guard will take the unexpended portion of Monday's rations, and full rations for Tuesday, with them.

6. The Transport Officer will arrange to have sufficient limbers at the duck-walk on Tuesday morning to take spare kit, blankets, company stores etc to the Q.M. stores.

7. 2/Lt Harvey will arrange to have the guns, spare parts boxes etc from G.H.Q., R Line taken to Voormezeele by 10 am on January 2nd without fail. One man from each gun position will remain as guides for 122nd M.G. Coy's garrison.

8. Full rations, with the exception of the breakfast ration, will be issued to all men before 7.30 am on 2nd inst by the C.Q.M.S.

9. Officers and N.C.Os are responsible that men of their Sections do not wander aimlessly about the village or the trenches during the relief, and all ranks must be as quick as possible in getting away from C.H.Q., at Voormezeele.

10. All huts, tents, cookhouses and latrines in QUEBEC CAMP will be left in a scrupulously clean condition. Pte Hamilton, R.A.M.C. will inspect the Camp thoroughly and report on its cleanliness to the Adjutant, before the Company leaves the Camp. A guard of 1 Cpl and 3 men will remain in the Camp until the 122nd M.G. Company take it over.

11. On completion of relief, wire "SURPRISE".

12. Acknowledge.

                              (sd) A.McKie Reid, Lt & Adjt
                                123rd Machine Gun Company.

In the Field,
   January 1st 1917.

To. 1 War Diary
    2 Duplicate   9 Xth Corps M.G.O.
    3 O.C. Section.1   10 123rd Infy Brigade
    4 "   "   2   11 122nd Machine Gun Coy
    5 "   "   3   12 122nd Infy Brigade.
    6 "   "   4
    7 2/Lt Harvey
    8 Transport Officer

Secret

**Operation Orders 15 By Captain C.F. Dingwall,
commanding 123rd Machine Gun Company.**

1. The 123rd M.G. Coy will be relieved by the 122nd M.G. Coy in the ST ELOI Sector on January 7th 1917.

2. The relieving Company is expected to be at C.H.Q at 10.30 am on the 7th, when guides from each gun team will conduct the relieving gun teams to their positions.

3. Section Officers will hand over all tripods, 10 filled belt boxes per gun, all trench stores and R.E. stores to the relieving Section, and obtain a signed receipt for same.

4. The guns of Sections 3 and 4 will be placed in the G.H.Q. R Line. Lt Hanson will send his four guns direct there, and report to C.H.Q. when they are in position. No.3 Section, on relief, will bring guns to C.H.Q. before taking to G.H.Q. Line.
The garrison of G.H.Q. Line will be composed of :-
   Cpl Keane and 3 men from No.1 Section
   1 L/cpl   and 3 men from No.2 Section
             4 men from No.3 Section
   1 L/cpl   and 3 men from No.4 Section
Section Officers will send the names of the men detailed to C.H.Q. by 8 am on January 7th.
2/Lt Shaw will be in command of G.H.Q. R Line garrison and will take over all stores, tripods etc.

5. On completion of relief, Sections will move back, under Section Officers, to QUEBEC CAMP.

6. The C.Q.M.S. will make arrangements with the Transport Officer to have all necessary stores etc taken over to QUEBEC CAMP, and will have a hot meal prepared for the Company on their arrival. The Company cooks will parade at C.H.Q. at 8 am on the 7th inst, They, together with the Tunnelling section, and one signaller will proceed immediately to QUEBEC CAMP.

7. Section Officers and N.C.Os are responsible that men do not wander aimlessly about the trenches or the village during the relief.

8. All billets, emplacements, dugouts, latrines etc must be left scrupulously clean. Pte Hamilton, R.A.M.C. will personally inspect all the above in the Sector, before relief, and report to the Adjutant on their cleanliness.

9. Separate orders are issued to Transport Officer.

10. This office will close at 3 pm at VOORMEZEELE, and open at the same time at QUEBEC CAMP.

11. On completion of relief, wire "ALTOGETHER".

12. Acknowledge.

                                (sd)   A. McKie Reid, Lt & Adjt
                                       123rd Machine Gun Company.

In the Field,
  6th January 1917.

To.   1 War Diary
      2. Duplicate   7 Transport Officer
      3 O.C. No.1 Section   8 2/Lt Harvey
      4   "   " 2   "   9 Xth Corps M.G.O.
      5   "   " 3   "   10 O.C. 122nd M.G. Coy
      6   "   " 4   "   11 123rd Infy Bde
                                     12 122nd "   "

SECRET

Operation Orders 16 by Captain C.F. Dingwall
commanding 123rd Machine Gun Company.
----

1. The garrison of the G.H.Q. R Line will be relieved tomorrow, 10th inst, the relief commencing at 10.30 a.m.

2. One Sergeant and seven men from No.3 Section, one Corporal, one L/Corporal and six men from No.4 Section, detailed elsewhere, will relieve. Lt Hanson will conduct these men to SCOTTISH WOOD, where they will be met by guides, detailed by 2/Lt Shaw, at 10.30 a.m.

3. The Transport Officer will arrange to have a half limber at the duck walk at 9 a.m. to carry mens' packs. This limber will wait at SCOTTISH WOOD for the outcoming garrison.
A horse and groom will be provided for Lt Hanson, at the same time.

4. The relieving officer will take over, and sign for, all guns, tripods, ammunition etc. A list will be sent to C.H.Q.

5. Iron rations, field dressings, gas helmets and steel helmets will be inspected by Lt Hanson before the relieving party leave QUEBEC CAMP.

6. The unexpended portion of the day's rations will be taken, and one blanket per man. The second blanket will be handed to Section Sergeant to be placed with the Section's blankets.

7. The relief will be reported complete by Lt Hanson on his return to Camp.

8. Acknowledge.

(sd) A. McKie Reid, Lt & Adjt,
123rd Machine Gun Company.

In the Field,
January 9th 1917.

To.
1 War Diary
2 Duplicate
3 Lt Hanson
4 2/Lt Shaw
5 Transport Officer
6 123rd Infantry Brigade.

SECRET

Operation orders 17 by Captain C.F. Dingwall,
commanding 123rd Machine Gun Company.
Ref: B.O.O.58, January 11th 1917.

1. The 123rd M.G. Coy will relieve the 122nd M.G. Coy in the St Eloi Sector, on January 14th 1917.

2. The relieving Unit will be at VOORMEZEELE at 10.30 am, when guides detailed from 122nd M.G. Coy, will conduct the relieving gun teams to their positions.

3. Officers and their Sections will take up the following positions in the Line:-
    2/Lt Webster   VOORMEZEELE DEFENCES
    2/Lt Shaw   RIGHT SECTOR
    2/Lt Harvey   BUS HOUSE GROUP
    Lt Hanson   SPOIL BANK GROUP.

4. Relieving Sections will take over ten filled belt boxes per gun, all tripods, stores (trench & R.E.). Section Officers will check, and sign for these, and send a list to H.Q.

5. The Transport Officer will arrange to have one limber at the duck-walk on the evening of the 13th, to take the guns to VOORMEZEELE. One sergeant and three men, detailed elsewhere, will accompany the guns as a guard. They will take with them the unexpended portion of the day's rations, and full rations for the 14th.

6. The Transport Officer will arrange to have sufficient limbers at the duck-walk at 8 am on Sunday, to take blankets, stores, spare kit etc to MICMAC CAMP, and to take Orderly Room stores to VOORMEZEELE.
Detailed orders will be issued to the T.O. later.

7. 2/Lt Shaw will arrange to have guns etc from G.H.Q. Line at VOORMEZEELE H.Q. at 10.30 am without fail.
One guide per gun from G.H.Q. Line will be left at SCOTTISH WOOD to conduct 122nd M.G. Coy's teams to their positions in G.H.Q. Line. On completion of G.H.Q. relief, all men will report to H.Q.

8. Full rations, with the exception of the breakfast ration, will be issued to all men before 7.30 am on the 14th inst by the C.Q.M.S., who will see that there is a sufficient tea ration for the remainder of the day.

9. All huts, tents, cookhouses, and latrines in QUEBEC CAMP will be left in a scrupulously clean condition. Pte Hamilton, R.A.M.C., will inspect the Camp and report on its cleanliness to the Adjutant, before the Company leaves the Camp. A guard of 1 N.C.O. & 3 men will remain in the Camp until the 122nd Coy take it over.

10. On completion of relief, wire "BULL RUSH".

11. Acknowledge.

(sd) A. McKie Reid, Lt & Adjt
123rd Machine Gun Company.

In the Field,
January 12th 1917.

To. 1. War Diary
     2. File (duplicate)   7. Transport Officer
     3. O.C. No.1 Section   8. 123rd Infy Bde.
     4. "   2   "   9. 122nd M.G. Coy
     5. "   3   "   10. 122nd Infy Bde
     6. "   4   "   11. Xth Corps. M.G.O.

SECRET

Operation Orders 15 by Captain C.F. Dingwall
commanding 123rd Machine Gun Company.

Ref: 123rd Inf: Bde: O.O. 60.

1. The 123rd Machine Gun Company will be relieved by the 122nd M.G. in the St Eloi Section on January 21st 1917.

2. The relieving Unit is expected to be at VOORMEZEELE at 10.30 am, when guides from each gun team detailed by Section Officers, will meet the relieving teams at H.Q., and conduct them to their positions in the line.

3. Section Officers will hand over all tripods, ten filled belt boxes per gun, all trench and R.E. stores to the relieving Sections. A signed receipt will be obtained for same.

4. Section officers will send a list of all trench stores etc, and all work done to C.H.Q., before 8 am on 21st inst.

5. The guns of Sections 1 and 2 will be placed in the G.H.Q. Line after relief, and teams will report at C.H.Q. beforehand. The garrison of G.H.Q. Line will be composed of :-
   Sgt Barton and 3 men from No.1 Section
   1 L/Cpl and 3 men from No.2 Section
   1   "   " 3 "   "   3   "
   4 men   "   4   "
Section Officers will send names of O.R. detailed, by 8 am tomorrow morning to G.H.Q.
Lt Hanson will be in command of G.H.Q. Line, and will take over all tripods, stores etc.

6. On completion of relief, Sections will move back to QUEBEC CAMP under Section Officers.

7. The C.Q.M.S. will arrange to have all necessary stores taken to QUEBEC CAMP tomorrow morning, and will arrange to have a hot meal prepared for the Company on their arrival.
The Company cooks will parade at C.H.Q. at 8 am, and together with one signaller, will proceed to QUEBEC CAMP immediately.

8. In view of the recent hostile shelling in the village of VOORMEZEELE, great care must be taken by every one not unduly to expose themselves during the relief, otherwise, shell fire may be attracted.

9. All billets, emplacements, dugouts and latrines, must be left scrupulously clean. Pte Hamilton, R.A.M.C., will personally inspect all the above in the Sector, and report to the Adjutant on their cleanliness.

10. Separate orders have been issued to Transport Officer.

11. On completion of relief, wire "THEODORE".

12. Acknowledge.

```
To. 1  WarDiary              (sd) A. McKie Reid,  Lt & Adjt
    2  Duplicate
    3  O.C. 1 Section        123rd Machine Gun Company.
    4   "   2    "
    5   "   3    "
    6   "   4    "
    7  Transport Officer
    8  122nd M.G. Coy
    9  123rd Inf. Bde
   10  Xth Corps M.G.O.
```

In the Field.   Jany 20th 1917.

2. Duplicate

Operation Orders 19 by Captain G. F. Dingwall,
commanding 123rd Machine Gun Company.

1. The garrison of the G.H.Q. 2nd line will be relieved on
   24th inst, commencing at 10.30 am.

2. The garrison relieving will be composed of :-

   1 Cpl & 4 men from No. 1 Section.
   1 Sgt & 4 men from No. 2 Section.
        4 men from No. 3 Section.
   1 L/c & 3 men from No. 4 Section.

   The Cpl will take charge of the left guns (Maxims).
   These men will be detailed elsewhere.
   2/Lt Webster will conduct these men to SCOTTISH WOOD, where
   they will be met by guides detailed by Lt. Hanson.

3. The Transport Officer will arrange to have a limber and an
   officer's horse with groom at the Duck-walk at 9 am.   This
   limber will wait at SCOTTISH WOOD to bring down the relieved
   garrison's packs.

4. Iron rations, field dressings, steel helmets and gas helmets
   and respirators will be inspected by 2/Lt Webster before the
   relieving party leaves QUEBEC CAMP.

5. The unexpended portion of the day's rations will be taken, and
   one blanket per man.   The second blanket will be handed to
   Section Sgt to be placed with Section's blankets.

6. The relief will be reported complete by 2/Lt Webster on his
   return to camp.

                                   (sd) A. McKie Reid, Lt & Adjt

                                         123rd Machine Gun Company.

In the Field,
   January 23rd 1917.

To.

   1 War Diary
   2 Duplicate
   3 Lt Hanson
   4 2/Lt Webster
   5 Transport Officer
   6 123rd Infy. Brigade.

SECRET

Operation Orders No by Captain C.F. Dingwall,
commanding 123rd Machine Gun Company.

1. The 123rd M.G. Coy will relieve the 122nd M.G. Coy in the ST ELOI Sector on the 27th inst.
The relieving Company will be at VOORMEZEELE at 10.30 am, and will be met by guides detailed from 122nd M.G. Coy.

2. Officers and their Sections will take up the following positions in the line.

    2/Lt Harvey   VOORMEZEELE DEFENCES
    2/Lt Shaw   BUS HOUSE GROUP
    2/Lt Webster   RIGHT GROUP
    Lt Hanson   SPOIL BANK GROUP.

3. Relieving Sections will take over, check, and sign for the usual stores, and will send a list to H.Q.

4. Lt Hanson will arrange to have the guns from G.H.Q. line brought to C.H.Q. by 10.30 am, leaving guides in SCOTTISH WOOD for the relieving garrison.

5. The Transport Officer will arrange to have a limber at the duck-walk on the evening of the 26th, to take guns to VOORMEZEELE. One sergeant and three men, detailed elsewhere, will accompany the guns as a guard. They will take with them the unexpended portion of the day's rations, and full rations for 27th.
The Transport Officer will also arrange to have sufficient limbers at the duck-walk at 8 am on 27th to take blankets, stores etc to Q.M.S. stores, and two limbers at 9 am to take mens' packs to DICKEBUSCH.
In the afternoon, sufficient transport must be at duck-walk to take Orderly Room stores etc to VOORMEZEELE.

6. Full rations, with the exception of the breakfast rations will be issued by C.Q.M.S. before 8 am on 27th. He will see that there is sufficient tea ration for the remainder of the day.

7. All tents, huts, cookhouses, latrines etc. in QUEBEC CAMP, must be left scrupulously clean. Pte Hamilton, R.A.M.C., will inspect the Camp and report on its cleanliness.
A guard of 1 N.C.O. and 3 men will remain in the Camp until 122nd M.G. Coy take it over.

8. Sections Sergeants will see that all men in their Sections rub whale oil on their feet before 8 am.

9. On completion of relief, wire "AUREA".

10. Acknowledge.

                        (sd) A. McKie Reid, Lt & Adjt
                        123rd Machine Gun Company.

In the Field,
January 26th 1917.

To.
1 War Diary
2 Duplicate
3 O.C. Section 1
4 "   "   2
5 "   "   3   9 Xth Corps. M.G.O.
6 "   "   4   10 123rd Inf Bde
7 Transport Officer   11 122nd
8 122nd M.G. Coy

Army Form C. 2118.

123rd MACHINE GUN COY

WAR DIARY or INTELLIGENCE SUMMARY for the month of FEBRUARY 1917

(Erase heading not required.)

Instructions regarding War Diaries and Intelligence Summaries are contained in F.S. Regs., Part II and the Staff Manual respectively. Title Pages will be prepared in manuscript.

Place	Date 1917 Feby:	Hour	Summary of Events and Information	Remarks and references to Appendices
Voormezeele	1		Trench troops	
Reninghelst	2		Relieved by 122 M.G.Coy in St Eloi Sector.	O.O.21
	3		Rest billets. Gun cleaning etc	
	4		" Bathing parade, clothing inspection, pay parade. Ptes.Williams (Artificer), Smith & Schofield joined Coy from Base.	O.O.22
	5		Inter-Coy relief G.H.Q. 2nd line.	
	6		Rest billets. Gun drill, stripping etc. Use of Brigade School for firing stoppages, from 12 noon to 2 pm.	
	7		Rest billets. Use of Brigade School for firing stoppages.	
	8		Rest billets. Gun drill and Route march during morning. Preparing guns etc for tour in line. During tour in rest attached men were given instruction on the gun. The C.O. tested them in combined drill. Their performance was very good.	
Voormezeele	9		Relieved 122 M.G.Coy in St Eloi Sector	O.O.23
	10&11		Trench troops	
	12		Trench troops. 2/Lt Williams attached to this Unit from 134th Coy M.G. Corps.	
	13&14		Trench troops	
	15		Trench troops	
Reninghelst	16		Relieved by 122 M.G. Coy in St Eloi Sector	O.O.24
	17 to 20		Rest billets. Camp inspected by Corps Commander, Lieut Genl.Moreland. Transport Lines by the Brigadier. Very good report about the animals. Brigade School used for firing stoppages.	
	19		Inter Coy relief of G.H.Q. 2nd Line. Pte Hollands joined Coy from Base.	
	20		Rest billets. At 6.15 pm dug-out in Scottish Wood blown up, 3 men killed, Ptes. Adair, Robson and Barker.	O.O.25
Voormezeele	21		Relieved 122 M.G. Coy in St Eloi Sector. 5.30 pm Dug-out in Crater Lane blown in, gun team commander killed, 1 man wounded. Pte Walton joined the Company from Base.	O.O.26
	22		Trench troops. Rebuilding dug-out at Crater Lane.	
	23		Trench troops. Emplacements visited by Xth Corps M.G.Officer. Gun blown up at No.7 emplacement.	

Army Form C. 2118.

WAR DIARY
or
INTELLIGENCE SUMMARY

(Erase heading not required.)

Instructions regarding War Diaries and Intelligence Summaries are contained in F. S. Regs., Part II. and the Staff Manual respectively. Title Pages will be prepared in manuscript.

Place	Date	Hour	Summary of Events and Information	Remarks and references to Appendices
	1917 Feby			
Voormezeele	24		Trench troops. Co-operation in daylight raid by 124th Infantry Bde.	
	25		Trench troops. Wiring round the FORT.	
Reninghelst	26		Relieved by 122 M.G. Coy in the St Eloi Sector.	O.O.27
	27		Rest billets. Bathing parade and clothing inspection. Revolver practice in afternoon.	
	28		Rest billets. Commanding Officer'sparade. Gun drill, stoppages, stripping etc. Ptes.Barnett, Britton, Brady & Andrews joined the Coy from the Base.	
GENERAL			The Company experienced bad luck during the month. - 4 other ranks killed, 1 wounded. 1 gun blown up. No case of trench feet has occurred in this Company so far. 7 O.ranks attended coursesduring the month, i.e. 2,Machine Gun Course, CAMIERS, 3, Course of Sanitation, BOESCHAEPE, 1, Course of Anti Aircraft at VLAMERTINGHE 1, Course of Grenades TERDEGHEM. Indirect fire was carried out during the tours in the line on the Enemy dumps, trenches, railways and dug-outs. 2 O.ranks were slightly wounded while building dug-outs. Promotions. Captain Dingwall to be Major, 2/Lts Webster, Harvey and Shaw to be-Lieutenants, dated 1.1.17.	

C.P.Dingwall Major.
Comndg 123 Coy M.G.C.

Secret

Copy I

Operation Order 21 by Captain G.F. Dingwall,
commanding 123rd Machine Gun Company.
Reference 123rd Inf Brigade O.O.62.

1. The 123rd M.G. Coy will be relieved by the 122nd M.G. Coy in the S.T. Eloi Sector on February 2nd 1917.

2. The relieving unit is expected to be at VOORMEZEELE at 10.30 am when guides from each gun team, detailed by Section officers, will meet the relieving teams and conduct them to their positions in the line.

3. Section officers will hand over all tripods, ten filled belt boxes per gun, all trench stores and R.E. stores to the relieving sections. A signed receipt will be obtained for same.

4. Section officers will send a list of all trench stores etc and all work done to C.H.Q. by 8 am on the 2nd inst.

5. The guns of sections 3 and 4 will be placed in the G.H.Q. 2nd line, after relief. The garrison of G.H.Q. line will be composed of
    Sgt Oates & 4 men from No.3 Section
    Cpl Donald 4 " 2 "
              4 " 1 "
              4 " 4 "
Section officers will send names of O.R. detailed by 8 am on the morning of the 2nd. 2/Lt Harvey will be in command of G.H.Q. line, and take over all stores, tripods etc.

6. On completion of relief, sections will move back to QUEBEC CAMP under Section officers.

7. The C.Q.M.S. will arrange to have all necessary stores taken to QUEBEC CAMP on the morning of the 2nd February. He will also arrange to have a hot meal prepared for the Company on their arrival at Camp.
The Company cooks and fatigue party will parade at C.H.Q. at 8 am on the 2nd February.

8. All billets, dugouts, latrines etc, will be left scrupulously clean.

9. Separate orders have been issued to the Transport Officer.

10. On completion of relief, wire "BLANCHE".

11. Acknowledge.

In the Field,   (sd)   S. Swett, Lieut,
  31st Jany 1917.
                                        123rd Machine Gun Company.

To. 1 War Diary
    2 Duplicate   7 Transport Officer
    3 O.C. No.1 Section   8 122nd M.G. Company
    4   "   2   "   9. 10th Corps M.G.O.
    5   "   3   "   10 123rd Infantry Brigade
    6   "   4   "   11 122nd Infantry Brigade

Operation Orders 22, by Captain G.F. Dingwell,
Commanding 123rd Machine Gun Company.

---

1. The garrison of the G.H.Q. 2nd Line will be relieved on the 5th inst commencing at 10.30 am.

2. The garrison relieving will be composed of :-

    Sgt Edden and 4 men from No.2 Section
    4 men from No.3 Section
    Cpl Thompson & 4 men from No.4 Section
    4 men from No.4 Section

    Cpl Thompson will take charge of the left sector (Moluse).
    The men will be detailed elsewhere.
    2/Lt Harvey will arrange for guides to meet the relieving teams.

3. The Transport Officer will arrange to have a limber at the duckboards at 9 am to take kits to DICKEBUSCH. The limber will wait for the relieved garrison.

4. Iron rations, Steel helmets, field dressings, respirators (box) will be inspected by the Orderly Officer before the garrison leaves QUEBEC CAMP.

5. The unexpended portion of the days rations will be taken and one blanket. Section sergeants will arrange to collect the second blanket.

6. The relief will be reported complete by message sent down by 2/Lt Harvey with senior N.C.O.

          (sd)   S. Scott,   Lieut,
          123rd Machine Gun Company.

In the Field,
 February 4th 1917.

To.   1   War Diary
    2   Duplicate
    3   2/Lt Harvey
    4   Transport Officer
    5   123rd Infantry Brigade.

Operation Orders No.23 by Capt G.F. Dingwall
commanding 123rd Machine Gun Company.

1. The 123rd M.G. Coy will relieve the 122nd M.G. Coy in the St Eloi Sector, on the 9th inst.

2. The relieving Company will be at VOORMEZEELE at 10.30 am and will be met by guides detailed by 122nd M.G. Coy.

3. The Officers and Sections will take up the following positions in the line:-
   2/Lt Shaw   Voormezeele Defences
   2/Lt Webster Right Sector
   2/Lt Harvey   Bus House Group
   Lt Hanson   Spoil Bank

4. The usual stores will be taken over, and signed for by the Section Officers and a copy sent to Company H.Q.

5. 2/Lt Harvey will arrange to have the guns from C.H.Q. 2nd line taken to C.H.Q., VOORMEZEELE by 10.30 am on the 9th inst.

6. Separate orders will be issued to Transport Officer and C.Q.M.S.

7. Full rations, with the exception of the breakfast ration will be issued by the C.Q.M.S. before 8 am on the 9th inst.

8. All huts, tents, cookhouses, latrines etc to be left scrupulously clean. Pte Hamilton, R.A.M.C., will inspect the Camp and report on its cleanliness. 1 N.C.O. and 3 men will remain in charge of the Camp until it is taken over by 122nd M.G. Coy.

9. Section sergeants will see that all men rub their feet with whale oil before 8 am on the 9th inst.

10. All steel helmets, respirator boxes, field dressings, iron rations etc will be inspected by Section Officer before moving off from QUEBEC CAMP.

11. On completion of relief, wire "CECILE".

12. Acknowledge.

(sd) S. Scott, Lieut
123rd Machine Gun Company.

In the Field,
February 7th 1917.

To. 1 War Diary
    2 Duplicate
    3 O.C. No.1 Section
    4   "   2   "
    5   "   3   "
    6   "   4   "
    7 Transport Officer
    8 Xth Corps M.G. Officer
    9 122nd Machine Gun Coy
   10 123rd Infantry Brigade
   11 122nd Infantry Brigade

SECRET

Operation Order No.24 by Captain C.F.Dingwall,
commanding 123rd Machine Gun Company.
Ref. Brigade O.O. No.64.

1. The 122nd M.G. Coy will relieve the 123rd M.G. Coy in the St Eloi Sector on the 16th instant.

2. The relieving Company will be at VOORMEZEELE at 10.30 am and will be met by guides detailed by 123rd M.G. Coy.

3. Section Officers will hand over, all tripods, ten filled belt boxes per gun, all trench and R.E. stores to the relieving sections. A receipt will be obtained for same.

4. Section Officers will send in to C.H.Q. by 8 am on the 16th inst, a list of trench stores, and all work done.

5. The guns of Sections 1 and 2 will be placed in the G.H.Q. 2nd Line after relief. The garrison will be as follows, under 2/Lt Webster :-

    4 men   from Section No.1
    4 "   "   "   2
    Cpl George & 4 men "   "   3
    Sgt Avis   & 4 "   "   "   4

    All trench stores, tripods etc will be taken over, and copy sent to C.H.Q. Section officers will send in names of men detailed for G.H.Q. 2nd line before 8 am on the 16th inst.

6. On completion of relief, sections will move back to QUEBEC CAMP under Section officers.

7. Separate orders issued to Transport Officer and CQMS re transport of stores, rations etc, to QUEBEC CAMP, on the 16th inst.

8. Company Cooks and a fatigue party will parade at C.H.Q., VOORMEZEELE, at 3 am on the 16th inst, and proceed to QUEBEC CAMP.

9. All billets, dugouts, latrines, cook-houses, emplacements etc will be left scrupulously clean.

10. On completion of relief, wire "DOROTHEA".

11. Acknowledge.

                              (sd)   S. Scott, Lieut
                                    123rd Machine Gun Company

In the Field,
  February 15th 1917.

To. 1 War Diary
     2 Duplicate
     3 O.C. Section 1
     4   "   " 2
     5   "   " 3
     6   "   " 4
     7 Transport Officer
     8 122nd M.G. Coy
     9 Xth Corps M.G.O.
    10 123rd Infantry Bde
    11 122nd   "   "

Operation Order 25 by Captain C.F. Dingwall,
commanding 123rd Machine Gun Company.

1. The garrison of G.H.Q. 2nd Line will be relieved on the 19th inst at 10.30 am.

2. The relieving garrison will be composed of :-
   Cpl Keane and 4 men from No.1 Section
                 4 "   "   "   2   "
                 4 "   "   "   3   "
   Sgt Whittaker 4 "   "   "   4   "
   2/Lt Webster will arrange for guides to meet the relieving teams.

3. The Transport Officer will arrange to have transport at Duck-walk at 9 am on the 19th inst, to take kits etc to DICKEBUSCH, and bring back those of the relieved garrison.

4. Iron rations, steel helmets, field dressings, respirator boxes etc will be inspected before leaving QUEBEC CAMP.

5. The unexpended portion of the days rations, and one blanket will be taken. Section Sergeants will arrange to collect the second blanket.

6. The relief will be reported complete by message sent down by senior N.C.O.

                                    (sd)   S. Scott,   Lieut,
                                           123rd Machine Gun Company.

In the Field,
February 18th 1917.

To.
    1 War Diary
    2 Duplicate
    3 2/Lt Webster
    4 Transport Officer
    5 123rd Infantry Brigade.

Operation Order 26 by Captain C.F. Dingwall,
Commanding 123rd Machine Gun Company.
----

1. The 123rd M.G. Coy will relieve the 122nd M.G. Coy in the St Eloi Sector on the 21st inst.

2. The relieving Company will be at VOORMEZEELE at 10.30 am and will be met by guides detailed by 122nd M.G. Coy.

3. The Officers and Sections will take up the following positions:-
    - 2/Lt Shaw   VOORMEZEELE
    - 2/Lt Harvey   Bus House
    - 2/Lt Webster   Right Sector
    - Lt Hanson   Spoil Bank

4. All stores etc will be signed for, and copy sent to G.H.Q.

5. 2/Lt Webster will arrange to have guns etc that are in G.H.Q. 2nd line to be at VOORMEZEELE at 10.30 am.

6. Separate orders to Transport Officer and CQMS.

7. Rations for tomorrow will be issued by the CQMS.

8. All huts, tents, cookhouses, latrines etc will be left scrupulously clean. Pte Hamber R.A.M.C. will inspect, and report on the cleanliness of the same.

9. A guard of 1 N.C.O. and 3 men will remain to hand over the Camp.

10. Section Sergeants will report that men have rubbed their feet with whale oil.

11. All steel helmets, box respirators, iron rations, field dressings etc, will be inspected by Section Officers before moving off from QUEBEC CAMP.

12. On completion of relief, wire "EDNA".

13. Acknowledge.

           (sd) S. Scott, Lieut
           123rd Machine Gun Company.

In the Field,
 20th February 1917.

To.
1. War Diary
2. Duplicate
3. Transport Officer
4. O.C. No.1 Section
5. " 2 "
6. " 3 "
7. " 4 "
8. Xth Corps M.G.O.
9. 122nd M.G. Coy
10. 123rd Infantry Brigade
11. 122nd Infantry Brigade
12. 2/Lt Williams.

Operation Orders 27 by Major C.F.Dingwall,
commanding 123rd Machine Gun Company.

1. The 122nd M.G. Coy will relieve the 123rd M.G. Coy in the St. Eloi Sector on the 26th inst.

2. The relieving Company will be at VOORMEZEELE at 10.30 am & will be met by guides.

3. Section officers will hand over, all tripods, ten filled belt boxes, ten unopened bulk S.A.A. boxes per gun, all trench & R.E. stores. A receipt will be obtained for same.

4. A list of trench stores to be handed over, and work done, will be sent to G.H.Q. by 8 am on the 26th inst.

5. The guns of Sections 1 and 4 will be placed in G.H.Q. 2nd Line and garrisoned as follows, under 2/Lt Williams.

    Sgt Swanston & 4 men   Section 1
    L/Cpl Hall   & 4 "   "   2
                    4 "   "   3
                    4 "   "   4

   All tripods, trench stores etc will be taken over and copy sent to G.H.Q. Section Officers will send in names of men detailed for G.H.Q. 2nd Line.

6. On completion of relief, Sections will move to QUEBEC CAMP under Section Officers.

7. Separate orders issued to Transport Officer and CQMS.

8. Company cooks and fatigue party will parade at G.H.Q. at 8 am on the 26th inst, and proceed to QUEBEC CAMP.

9. All billets, dug-outs, latrines, cookhouses, emplacements etc, to be left scrupulously clean.

10. On completion of relief, wire "GOLORA".

11. Acknowledge.

                                    (sd)   S. Scott, Lieut
                                           123rd Machine Gun Company.

In the Field,
    February 25th 1917.

To.   1 War Diary
      2 Duplicate
      3 O.C. Section 1
      4   "   "   2
      5   "   "   3
      6   "   "   4
      7 Transport Officer
      8 123rd Infantry Brigade
      9 122nd Infantry Brigade
     10 122nd M. G. Company
     11 Xth Corps M. G. Officer.

Army Form C. 2118.

123rd Machine Gun Coy

WAR DIARY
or
INTELLIGENCE SUMMARY

(Erase heading not required.)

for the month of MARCH 1917.

Place	Date 1917	Hour	Summary of Events and Information	Remarks and references to Appendices
Reninghelst	March 1		Rest billets. Gun drill, stripping & instruction. Big percentage of Company inoculated. Lt Webster to Hospital.	
	2		Inter-Company relief of G.H.Q. 2nd line. Inspection of Transport by Divl.Commdr. Very pleased with the M.G. transport. Lost first place for best turnout by 1½ points.	O.O.28
	3		Rest Billets. Instructions & points before firing. Route march in afternoon.	
Voormezeele	4		Relieved 122nd M.G.Coy in St.Eloi Sector.	O.O.29
	5		Trench troops. Wiring emplacements. Bullet jammed in barrel. Bulged barrel, putting gun completely out of action. 2/Lt Agate joined from Base.	
	6		Trench troops. Divl. Genl. round the lines. Wiring.Sgt D-Cox wounded.	
	7		Trench troops. Wiring. Company H.Q. shelled. Lt Doherty left Company for Cavalry Branch.	
	8		Trench troops. 2 guns moved from Voormezeele Defences to the BLUFF.	O.O.30
	9		Trench troops. Wiring. Fired occasional 'tracer' bullets., during indirect fire.	
Reninghelst	10		Relieved by 122nd M.G.Coy in St. Eloi Sector. 2/Lt Acason joined from Base.	O.O.31
	11		Rest billets. Church, Bathing and clothing parades.	
	12		Rest billets. Fire stoppages on the range. Instruction in gun drill stripping etc.	
	13		Inter-Company relief of G.H.Q. 2nd Line. Bathing parade for the relieved men.	O.O.32
	14		Rest billets. Route march.	
	15		Rest billets. Bombing instruction in the morning. Gas shell demonstration in the afternoon.	
Voormezeele	16		Relieved 122nd M.G.Coy in St. Eloi Sector.	O.O.33
	17		Trench troops. Divl.Genl round the line. Wiring emplacements, Indirect fire. 2/Lt Russell-Jones joined from Base.	
	18		Trench troops. Wiring emplacements. Indirect fire was carried out.	
	19		Trench troops. Wiring emplacements. Indirect fire carried out. Bde Commdr round the lines. 2/Lt Edlings joined from 116th Company.	

WAR DIARY
or
INTELLIGENCE SUMMARY

(Erase heading not required.)

Army Form C. 2118

Instructions regarding War Diaries and Intelligence Summaries are contained in F. S. Regs., Part II. and the Staff Manual respectively. Title Pages will be prepared in manuscript.

Place	Date 1917	Hour	Summary of Events and Information	Remarks and references to Appendices
Voormezeele	March 20		Trench troops. Wiring emplacements. Indirect fire was carried out. Bde Commdr round the lines.	
	21		Trench troops. Wiring emplacements. Indirect fire was carried out on usual targets.	
Reninghelst	22		Relieved by 122nd M.G.Coy in St Eloi Sector. 2/Lt Leach joined Coy.	O.O.34
	23		Rest billets. Bathing, clothing & pay parades. Stand to.	
	24		Rest billets. Route march. gun drill etc.	
	25		Rest billets. Church parade. Divl Commdrs parade for distribution of medal ribbons. Inter-Company relief of G.H.Q 2nd Line. under 2/Lt Acason. Inspection of Transport by Divl Commdr.Complimented Coy on condition of mules.	O.O.35
	26		Rest billets. Lecture by Brigadier in the morning. Supplied fatigue party for the new Camp.	
	27		Rest Billets. Moved into New Camp at MICMAC.	
	28		Rest Billets. Lt.A.McK.Reid rejoined from sick leave.	
Voormezeele	29		Relieved 122nd M.G. Coy in St Eloi Sector.	O.O.36
	30		Trench troops "	
	31		" "	

GENERAL REMARKS

During the month much work was done in the way of repairing trenches making emplacements, and wiring in front of same.
A considerable influx of new officers (6) joined the Company during the month after the Company had managed with so few for so many months.
The weather during the latter part of the month has been very inclement, yet the health of the Company has kept up to its normal.

Commdg 123rd M. G. Coy
Major

Operation Orders 28 by Major C.F.Dingwall,
commanding 123rd Machine Gun Company.
----

1. The garrison of G.H.Q. 2nd Line will be relieved on the 2nd inst at 10.30 am.

2. The following will form the new garrison:-
   Sgt Mackie & 4 men from Section. 3.
   Cpl Thompson 4 " " " 4.
   4 " " " 2.
   4 " " " 1.
   2/Lt Williams will arrange guides.

3. Transport Officer will arrange for transport to be at duck-walk at 9 am for packs etc, and horse for officer.

4. Iron rations, steel helmets, field dressings, respirator boxes etc, will be inspected by Lieut Hanson before the party moves off.

5. The unexpended portion of the days rations and one blanket will be taken. The second blanket will be collected by Section sergeants.

6. Completion of relief will be reported by Lieut Hanson on arrival back in Camp.

(sd) S. Scott, Lieut
123rd Machine Gun Company.

In the Field,
1.3.1917.

To. 1 War Diary
    2 Duplicate
    3 2/Lt Williams
    4 Transport Officer
    5 123rd Infantry Bde.

Operation Orders 29 by Major C.F. Dingwall,
commanding 123rd Machine Gun Company.
----

1. The 123rd M.G. Company will relieve the 122nd M.G. Company in the St Eloi Sector on the 4th inst.

2. The relieving Company will be at VOORMEZEELE at 10.30 am, and will be met by guides.

3. Officers and Sections will take up the same positions as before.

4. All stores etc will be signed for, and copy sent to C.H.Q.

5. 2/Lt Williams will arrange for guns in G.H.Q. 2nd Line to be at VOORMEZEELE at 10.30 am, 4th inst.

6. Separate orders to Transport Officer.

7. C.Q.M.S. will arrange rations for the 4th inst.

8. All huts, tents, cookhouses, latrines etc to be left scrupulously clean. Pte Hamber will report on cleanliness of the Camp.

9. A guard of 1 N.C.O. and 3 men will remain and hand over the Camp.

10. All men will rub their feet with whale oil by 8 am on the 4th inst. Section Sergeants will report that this has been done.

11. All steel helmets, box respirators, iron rations etc will be inspected by Section Officers before moving off.

12. On completion of relief, wire "HAZEL".

13. Acknowledge.

            (sd) S. Scott, Lieut
            123rd Machine Gun Company.

In the Field,
 3rd March 1917.

To. 1. War Diary
   2. Duplicate
   3. O.C. Section 1
   4. " " 2
   5. " " 3
   6. " " 4
   7. Transport Officer
   8. 123rd Inf: Bde.
   9. 122nd " "
  10. 122nd M.G. Coy.
  11. Xth Corps M.G.O.

Operation Orders 30 by Major G.F. Dingwall,
commanding 123rd Machine Gun Company.

1. On the 8th instant, the guns at Convent Lane Extension and Convent will be changed to Gordon's Post and Gun Alley in The Bluff.

2. Two guns from G.H.Q. 2nd Line, 122nd M.G. Coy will relieve these two guns.

3. All belt boxes, boxes bombs, very lights, Petrol tins, trench boots, shovels, picks, braziers will be taken to the new positions.

4. All bulk S.A.A., Vermoral sprayers will be handed over to Officer i/c G.H.Q. 2nd Line, 122nd M.G. Coy.

5. Fatigue party will be found from remaining two gun teams of No.2 Section.

6. Lt Shaw will move to Spoil Bank. The two teams and fatigue party will report to Officer's dugout, Spoil Bank by 2 pm Lt Hanson will guide teams to their respective positions. The remaining two guns of No.2 Section will come under orders of H.Q.

7. Rations have been arranged for.

8. Code word on completion of relief "IRENE".

(sd) S. Scott, Lieut
123rd M. G. Company.

In the Field,
   7.2.1917.

No. 1 War Diary
   2 Duplicate
   3 O.C. 1&3 Sections
   4 " 2 "
   5 " 4 "
   6 123rd Inf Bde
   7 O.C. 122nd M.G. Coy
   8 Officer i/c G.H.Q. Line
   9 Corps M.G. Officer.

Operation Order 31 by Major C.F.Dingwall
commanding 123rd Machine Gun Company.
----

1. The 122nd M.G. Coy will relieve the 123rd M.G. Coy in the St Eloi Sector on the 10th inst.

2. The relieving Company will be at Voormezeele at 10.30 am and will be met by guides.

3. Section Officers will hand over all tripods, ten belt boxes, 10 boxes bulk S.A.A. per gun, all trench and R.E. stores. A receipt will be obtained.

4. Work done and list trench stores in pro forma will be sent into C.H.Q. by 8 am on the 10th inst.

5. The guns of Sections 2 and 3 will be in G.H.Q. 2nd line and garrisoned as follows under Lt Shaw :-
             4 men from Section 1.
             4 men   "   "   2.
     Cpl Woulidge & 4 men from Section 3.
     Sgt Whitaker & 4 "   "   "   4.
   A receipt will be given for all trench stores etc and copy sent to C.H.Q. Section Officers will send in list of men detailed for G.H.Q. 2nd Line.

6. On completion of relief, sections will move to Quebec Camp <u>under Section Officers.</u>

7. Separate orders to Transport Sergeant.

8. Company cooks and fatigue party will parade at C.H.Q. at 8am on the 10th inst and proceed to Quebec Camp.

9. All billets, dugouts, emplacements, cookhouses, latrines etc will be left scrupulously clean.

10. On completion of relief, wire "IRENE".

11. Acknowledge.

In the Field,   (sd) S. Scott, Lieut

   9th March 1917.   123rd M.G.Coy.

To. 1 War Diary
    2 Duplicate
    3 O.C. Section 1
    4   "   "   2
    5   "   "   3
    6   "   "   4
    7 Transport Officer
    8 123rd Infantry Bde
    9 122nd   "   "
   10 122nd M.G.Coy
   11 Xth Corps M.G.Officer.

<u>For information of O.C. 122nd M.G.Coy</u>

       Relief of Sections will be as follows.

       No.3 Section   5 6 7 10   gun positions
       No. 1   "   8 9 11 12
       No. 4   "   13 14 15 16   "   "
       No. 2   "   Gun Alley & Gordon's Post.
       Handed over with H.Q's No.4 & Fort.

Operation Orders 32 by Major G.F. Dingwall
commanding 123rd Machine Gun Company.
----

1. The garrison of the G.H.Q. 2nd line will be relieved on the 13th at 10.30 am.

2. The following will form the new garrison:-
   Cpl Baker and 6 men from No.1 Section
                   6 " "   2 "
   Sgt Oates " 6 " "   3 "
                   6 " "   4 "

   Lieut Shaw will arrange guides.

3. Transport Officer will arrange for transport to be at Duckwalk at 9 am for packs etc and a horse and mounted groom for the officer.

4. Iron rations, steel helmets, field dressings, box respirators etc will be inspected by 2/Lt Agate before the party moves off.

5. The unexpended portion of the days rations and one blanket will be taken. The second blanket will be collected by Section Sergeants.

6. Completion of relief will be reported by 2/Lt Agate on his return to Camp.

(sd) M.J.V. Hanson, Lieut
123rd Machine Gun Coy

In the Field,
   March 12th 1917.

1. War Diary
2. Duplicate
3. Lt Shaw
4. 2/Lt Agate
5. Transport Officer
6. 123rd Infy Bde.

Operation Order No.33 by Major C.F.Dingwall
commanding 123rd Machine Gun Company.

1. The 123rd M.G. Coy will relieve the 122nd M.G. Coy in the ST ELOI Sector on the 16th instant.

2. The relieving Company will be at VOORMEZEELE at 10.30 am and will be met by guides.

3. Officers and Sections will take up the same positions as before.

4. All stores etc will be signed for and copy sent to C.H.Q.,

5. Lieut Shaw will arrange to have guns in G.H.Q. 2nd Line at VOORMEZEELE by 10.30 am, 16th instant.

6. Separate Orders to Transport Officer.

7. C.Q.M.S. will arrange rations for the 16th inst.

8. All huts, tents, cookhouses, latrines etc to be left scrupulously clean. Pte Hamber will report on cleanliness of the Camp.

9. A guard of 1 N.C.O. and 3 men will remain and hand over the Camp to Adjutant.

10. All men will rub their feet with whale oil by 8 am, 16th inst, under Section Officers.

11. All steel helmets, box respirators, iron rations etc will be inspected by Section Officers before moving off.

12. On completion of relief, wire "KOLOMA".

13. Acknowledge.

                        (sd) M.J.V. Hanson, Lieut,

                              123rd Machine Gun Company.

In the Field,
   14th March 1917.

To.
1. War Diary
2. Duplicate
3. O.C. Section 1.
4. "   "   2
5. "   "   3
6. "   "   4
7. Transport Officer.
8. 123rd Infantry Brigade
9. 122nd Infantry Brigade
10. Corps Machine Gun Officer.
11. 122nd Machine Gun Company.

Operation Order No.34 by Major C.F.Dingwall
Commanding 123rd Machine Gun Company.

1. The 123rd M.G. Coy will be relieved by the 122nd M.G. Coy on the 22nd inst. in the ST ELOI Sector.

2. The relieving Company will be at VOORMEZEELE at 10.30 am and will be met by guides.

3. Section Officers will hand over tripods, ten filled belt boxes, 10 boxes bulk S.A.A. per gun. All trench and R.E. stores. A receipt will be obtained.

4. Work done and list of trench stores in pro forma will be sent to C.H.Q. by 8 am on the 22nd inst.

5. The guns of Nos. 1 and 4 Sections will be in G.H.Q. 2nd line, and garrisoned as follows under 2/Lt Agate and 2/Lt Acason:-
   Sgt Horridge, Cpl Keane and 6 men from No.1 Section
                             6   "   "   2 "
                             6   "   "   3 "
                             6   "   "   4 "
   A receipt will be given for all trench stores etc and copy sent to C.H.Q. Section Officers will send in list of men detailed for G.H.Q. 2nd Line by 8 am 22nd inst. No 4 Section will put two of their guns in ECLUSE trench and CANAL BANK on being relieved.

6. On completion of relief, Sections will move to QUEBEC CAMP under Section Officers.

7. Separate Orders to Transport Officer.

8. Company cooks and fatigue party, detailed elsewhere will parade at C.H.Q. at 8 am on the 22nd inst and move to QUEBEC CAMP.

9. All billets, dugouts, emplacements, cookhouses, latrines etc to be left scrupulously clean, special forms for which are enclosed.

10. On completion of relief, wire "LENA".

11. Acknowledge.

                                          (sd) M.J.V. Hanson, Lieut
                                          123rd Machine Gun Company.

In the Field,
21st March 1917.

To. 1. War Diary
      2. Duplicate
      3. O.C. No.1 Section.
      4.   "   2   " & Actg O.C. 4 Section.
      5.   "   3   "
      6.   "   "   " 2/Lt Agate.
      7. Transport Officer.
      8. 123rd Infantry Bde.
      9. 122nd
    10. 122nd M. G. Coy
    11. Xth Corps CMGO.

Operation Order 35 by Major C.F.Dingwall,
Commanding 123rd Machine Gun Company.

1. The garrison of the G.H.Q. 2nd Line will be relieved tomorrow the 25th at 4 pm.

2. The following will form the new garrison under 2/Lt Acason.

                       6 men from Section 1.
   L/Sgt Philip   and   6   "   "   "   2.
                             6   "   "   "   3.
   Cpl Wilson   and   6   "   "   "   4.

2/Lt Agate will arrange guides.

3. The Transport Officer will arrange for transport to be at Duckwalk at 2.30 pm for packs etc, also a horse and mounted groom for officer.

4. Iron rations, steel helmets, box respirators etc will be inspected by 2/Lt Acason before moving off.

5. The unexpended portion of the day's ration will be taken, also one blanket. The second blanket will be handed to the Section Sergeants.

6. Completion of relief will be reported by 2/Lt Agate on return to Camp.

After Order

The relieving party will receive clothing, necessaries, etc on the way up to the trenches.

                             (sd)   M.J.V. Hanson,   Lieut

                                 123rd Machine Gun Company.

In the Field,
   March 24th 1917.

To.   1.   War Diary
        2.   Duplicate
        3.   2/Lt Agate
        4.   2/Lt Acason
        5.   Transport Officer
        6.   123rd Infantry Brigade.

Operation Orders No.36 by Major C.F.Dingwall
commanding 123rd Machine Gun Company.
----

1. The 123rd M.G.Coy will relieve the 122nd M.G.Coy in the St Eloi Sector on the 29th inst.

2. The relieving Company will be at Voormezeele at 10.30 am and will be met by guides.

3. Officers and Sections will take up the following positions:-

   Section 1. Positions 8, 9, 11 and 12.
   " 2. Gordon's Post, Gun Alley, Canal Bank Extension, and No.16.
   " 3. Positions 5, 6, 7 and 10.
   " 4. Positions 13, 14, 15 and Oesthoek Farm.
   All stores etc will be signed for and a copy sent to C.H.Q.

4. 2/Lt Acason will arrange to have the guns now in G.H.Q. 2nd Line at Voormezeele by 10.30 am on the 29th inst.

5. Separate Orders to Transport Officer.

6. The C.Q.M.S. will arrange rations for the 29th inst.

7. All huts, tents, cookhouses, latrines etc to be left scrupulously clean. Pte Bamber will report on the cleanliness of the Camp.

8. All men will rub their feet with whale oil by 8 am on the 29th inst, under Section Officers.

9. All steel helmets, box respirators, iron rations etc will be inspected by Section Officers before moving off.

10. On completion of relief, wire "MADGE".

12. Acknowledge.

                                    (sd)   S. Scott,   Lieut
                                         123rd Machine Gun Company.

In the Field,

   March 27th 1917.

To. 1 War Diary
     2 Duplicate
     3 O.C. Section 1
     4   "   "   2
     5   "   "   3
     6   "   "   4
     7 Transport Officer
     8 2/Lt Acason
     9 123rd Infantry Brigade.
    10 122nd   "
    11 122nd M. G. Company
    12 Xth Corps M. G. Officer.

Army Form C. 2118.

123 M.G.Coy Vol XI

WAR DIARY
or
INTELLIGENCE SUMMARY

(Erase heading not required.)

Instructions regarding War Diaries and Intelligence Summaries are contained in F. S. Regs., Part II. and the Staff Manual respectively. Title Pages will be prepared in manuscript.

Place	Date	Hour	Summary of Events and Information	Remarks and references to Appendices
Voormezeele.	Apl/16 1		Trench troops. Wiring emplacements. Enemy shelling of back areas very heavy.	
	2&3		Trench troops. Wiring emplacements.Front quiet. CoyH.Qrs shelled. 1 direct hit.	
Micmac	4		Relieved by 122nd M.G.Coy in St Eloi Sector. Lt Reid 2 days tactical course under Xth Corps G.S.O.2.	O.O.37
	5		Rest Camp. Inoculation, clothing & kit inspection. Relief of G.H.Q Line by 124th M.G. Coy	O.O.38 O.O.39
On march	6		Marched to Steenvoorde via Abeele. Billeted at Steenvoorde at night.	
	7		Marched to Arneke via Cassel.Billeted at Arneke,Nord, at night.	
	8		Marched to Hellebroucq via Watten & Ganspette. Billeted in Chateau d'Hellebroucq	
Hellebroucq. Pas de Calais	9		Kit inspection, clothing parade etc.	
	10		Lieut Reypert joined Coy as Transport Officer.	
	11		Tactical Schemes.Pack saddle drill, gun drill etc.	
	12		Firing on short range. Indication & recognition of targets.	
	13		Sections joined Inf. Battns for tactical exercise - Practising attack.	
	14		Field firing on range	
	15		Church parades, clothing inspection.	
	16		Tactical exercises with Infantry.	
	17		Tactical exercises ordered, but postponed on account of weather.	
	18		Checking spare parts, cleaning guns etc.	
	19&20&21		Tactical exercises carried out with Infantry Battalions.	
	22		Church parades.Lt Russell-Jones proceeded on 2 days Tactical course under G.S.O.2. 2/Lt Eddings left Coy to proceed to Cavalry Branch, M.G.C. at Uckfield.	
On march	23		Left Hellebroucq. Marched with Brigade as advanced guard. 1 Section with vanguard, 3 Sections with main guard, via Watten to Arneke, Nord, where billeted for night.	O.O.40
	24		Left, Arneke and marched via Cassel & Steenvoorde. Billeted on Cassel -Steenvoorde road at corner of Terdeghem road.	
	25		Marched from Steenvoorde via Abeele to Reninghelst.	
Reninghelst Quebec Camp	26		Inspection of kits,boots,gas helmets etc., 24 men attached from Infantry Battalions, returned to units.	

Army Form C. 2118

WAR DIARY
or
INTELLIGENCE SUMMARY

(Erase heading not required.)

Instructions regarding War Diaries and Intelligence Summaries are contained in F. S. Regs., Part II. and the Staff Manual respectively. Title Pages will be prepared in manuscript.

Place	Date	Hour	Summary of Events and Information	Remarks and references to Appendices
Reninghelst Quebec Camp	Apl.17 27		Re-clothing of Company	
	28		2/Lt Acason proceeded on 3 day Tactical Course under Xth Corps G.S.O.2	
	29		Church Parade. Bombardment of neighbourhood of Camp by 9 in Armour piercing shells from 3 pm until 2 am 30th. Lt Hanson & Lt Harvey and 1 N.C.O. & 1 man proceeded to Camiers on a m.g. course.	
	30		Route March in morning. Gun cleaning etc in afternoon.	
			General	
			The Company has only been in the trenches for 4 days in this month. Other time spent in rest and training for the offensive, has appreciably improved the health and general condition of the Company.	
			Owing to the grant of 24 attached men to the Company, it was found that several additional employed men could be found, such as, boot repairer, tailor, forage man in transport etc, which tended to promote the efficiency of the Coy, and which, hitherto, owing to shortage of men had not been possible. These men having been ordered to return to their units, these employments have had to be abandoned.	

Christph.
Major
Commanding 123rd Machine Gun Company.

March Orders (Operation Order 40) by Major C.F.
Dingwall Commdg 123rd Coy, M.G. Corps.
Ref 123rd I.Bde. O.O. No.18. Ref Map Haz.5a.

1. The 123rd Coy M.G.C. will march from Hellebroucq to Arneke on 23rd instant.
   The 123rd Infantry Brigade will march as an advance guard. In accordance with this, No.3 Sec will march with the vanguard and will pass the starting point at the Cross Roads L.14 c 4.9 E end Watten (ref Map Sheet 27a N.E. at 8.11 am following the 20th D.L.I. and 1 Batty 190th Bde R.F.A. O.C. 3 Section will report to O.C. 20th D.L.I. on the march.
   The remaining 3 Sections will pass the starting point at 9.16 am leaving H.Q. at 8 am.
   No.3 Section will leave H.Q. at 7 am

2. 2 fighting limbers will accompany No.3 Section. The remainder of the transport will be drawn up as a whole and follow immediately behind the Company.

3. The Sections will pack their fighting limbers at ½ hourly intervals from 6.15 am.
   No.1 Section commencing at 6.15 am
   2 " " 6.30 am
   4 " " 6.45 am
   3 " will pack its fighting limbers tonight.

4. The C.Q.M.S. will arrange to have rations issued before breakfast. All meat ration must be cooked, and bully beef minced previously. Cooked beef in bulk will be carried in bulk in H.Q. limber, rear portion, and issued at the dinner halt. No.3 Section will take meat with it.

5. A motor lorry will be provided to carry blankets (which must be rolled and labelled by Sections), and packs which must be clearly marked with the owners name on the back. The packs of the drivers will also be placed on the lorry.
   Sec. Officers, the T.O. and the C.S.M. will personally inspect all packs and see that this is done.
   Sgt Barton and Pte McArdle will accompany the motor lorry and will be responsible for the unpacking and guarding of the contents at the Company billet at Arneke. No other men will ride on any vehicle.

6. A & B limbers   Q.M. stores
   C limber   at O.C disposal.
   D   Transport fore section
                     Officers' mess rear portion.
   H.Q.   Orderly Room - fore portion
                     Rations & dixies - rear portion
   The C.S.M. will detail Pte Barry to tie all spare dixies to limbers.

7. The T.O. will see that all food is in nosebags and all hay for chaff is cut, and the remainder is placed in hay nets. No bulk fodder whatever is to be placed in any limber.

8. Dress Fighting kit. Water bottles full. Steel helmets slung from left shoulder. Water proof sheets folded under flap of haversack. Men undergoing F.P. No.1 will carry full packs.

9. All billets must be left scrupulously clean. Section Officers will see to this, and that no personal or Company property is left in any billets. The C.S.M. will detail Pte Hamber RAMC to visit all billets, cookhouses, latrines etc before 7.45 am and report on their cleanliness to the Adjutant.

10. The C.Q.M.S. will detail L/c Taylor RAMC to see that the water cart is completely filled after the water bottles of the Coy have been filled.

P.T.O.

(2)

11. Section Officers will be responsible for checking their gun stores daily on completion of the march, reporting the same to the Adjutant. All fighting limbers will be cleaned nightly by the Sections.
Nos. 1 & 2 Sections will be responsible for cleaning all H.Q. limbers on evening of 23rd and Nos. 3 & 4 on evening of 24th.

12. Lieut Shaw will proceed to the Cross Roads at Le Menegat to be there at 10 am for the purpose of billeting the Company. He will leave H.Q. at 7.30 am.

(sd) A. McK. Reid, Lt & Adjt

123rd Machine Gun Company.

22.4.1917.

To.
1. War Diary
2. File
3. O.C. Sec. 1
4. "   "   2
5. "   "   3
6. "   "   4
7. T.O.
8. C.S.M.
9. QMS.
10 123rd I. Bde
11 M.G.O. Xth Corps.

March Orders by Major C.F. Dingwall,
commanding 123rd Machine Gun Company.   No.39.

Detail.   Orderly Officer 2/Lt Agate.   Reveille. 5.15 am.

1. The 123rd Machine Gun Company will move from Micmac Camp to Steenvoorde, starting at 9.40 am on the 6th inst.

2. All fighting limbers will be packed by 8 am. Breakfast 7.45 am.

3. The Signalling Corporal will detail 1 signaller to be at Reninghelst Church at 7 am to conduct one Motor Lorry which will be there, to the Machine Gun Camp at Micmac.

4. All blankets will be rolled, labelled, and taken down to the C.Q.M. stores by 7.15 am. All packs to be ready at the same hour. No man will put sandbags of personal kits on any limber.

5. Corporal Baker and 2 men of No.3 Section will proceed with the Motor Lorry to Steenvoorde and dump the blankets and packs at the most convenient spot to the Machine Gun billets.

6. Section Officers and Sub-Section Officers will take their kits in their fighting limbers.

7. The Orderly Room boxes will be in the fore portion of D Limber and the Officers' Mess boxes in the rear portion.

8. The C.Q.M.S. will arrange with the Transport Sergeant to detail all stores to go to Chippewa Camp.

9. Reference Operation Order No.38, the Transport Sergeant and drivers of Nos.1 and 3 limbers will remain behind to fetch guns and packs from G.H.Q. Line.

10. There will be 6 dixies in the rear portion of H.Q. Limber, and the remainder will be scattered. All belt boxes will be packed in Ammunition Carriers, under Section Officers.

11. All men will carry their steel helmets on their left shoulder. They will be in fighting order with haversack on back and canteens in canteen covers strapped to the haversack.

12. The C.Q.M.S. will arrange for the 6 rifles of the guard to be put in the rifle racks of the limbers.

13. All water bottles will be filled by 7 am, and L/Cpl Taylor will arrange to have the water cart again filled by 9 am.

14. The C.Q.M.S. will have available for the Q.M.stores, A and B limbers. C Limber will be at the disposal of the O.C.

15. Lieut Scott will go forward and will arrange for billetting at Steenvoorde at 10 am, under arrangements made by the Staff Captain.

16. The Transport Officer will see that the Transport Lines and the two huts of the Transport are left scrupulously clean and will hand in an inventory to Headquarters before 7 am.

17. Orderly Officer will make an inventory with Sgt Philip of the whole of the Camp and C.Q.M. stores.

18. Lieut Hanson will remain behind to hand over the Camp from the inventories of the Orderly Officer and Transport Officer.

19. The Transport Officer will arrange that the mess cart and all limbers are grouped on the road opposite H.Q. of Micmac Camp by 6.45 am. Drivers packs will be in their own limbers.

20. Waterproof sheets will be folded in the orthodox manner under the flap of the valise.

(sd) C.F.Dingwall, Major
Commanding 123rd Machine Gun Company.

April 5th 1917

Operation Orders 38 by Major C.F. Dingwall
commanding 123rd Machine Gun Company.
----

1. The 123rd M.G.Coy will be relieved by the 124th M.G.Coy in the St Eloi Sector on the 5th inst, relief to be complete by 4 pm on that date. Place for guides will be arranged later.

2. Os.C. 1 and 2 Sections will personally take the officers of 124th M.G.Coy round the emplacements, and explain every detail.

3. Each emplacement will be left with a range card, reserve gun orders, and a proper latrine.

4. All emplacements, dugouts and latrines to be left scrupulously clean before relief.

5. On completion of relief, all guns and all packs will be brought to Voormezeele and will remain in charge of Lt Harvey, 1 N.C.O. and 1 man, until Transport arrives to take the same to Steenvoorde via Route March.
Lt Shaw will march the remainder to Steenvoorde via route to be detailed later.

6. The Transport Officer will arrange that the Transport Sergeant remains with limbers 1 and 3 to carry guns and packs on the 5th instant to Steenvoorde after dark.

7. The food will be arranged at a place en route. Horses will be provided for Lieuts Shaw and Harvey.

8. Separate orders to Transport Officer.

9. On completion of relief, Lieut Shaw will wire "OLGA" to 123rd Infantry Brigade.

                                (sd) S. Scott, Lieut
                                123rd Machine Gun Company.

In the Field,
April 3rd 1917.

To.   1 War Diary
        2 Duplicate
        3 Lieut Shaw
        4 " Harvey
        5 Transport Officer
        6 123rd Infantry Bde
        7 122nd M. G. Coy
        8 124th M. G. Coy
        9 Xth Corps M.G.O.

Operation Orders No.37 by Major C.F.Dingwall
commanding 123rd Machine Gun Company.
----

1. The 123rd M.G. Coy will be relieved by the 122nd M.G. Coy in the St Eloi Sector on the 4th inst.

2. The relieving Company will be at Voormezeele at 10.30 am and will be met by guides, one from each team.

3. Section Officers will hand over all trench stores, a list of which will be sent down in pro forma without fail by 8 am to C.H.Q. on the 4th inst.

4. The guns of Sections 1 and 2 will be in the G.H.Q. 2nd Line under Lieuts Shaw and Harvey.

5. The Gun Team Commanders and 3 men from 1 and 2 Sections will be the garrison for the G.H.Q. 2nd Line.

6. Os.C. 1 and 2 Sections will send down a nominal roll of the men who are not going to garrison the G.H.Q. 2nd Line by 8 am on the 4th instant.

7. O.C. 1 Section will have the 2 guns in G.H.Q. 2nd Line, Convent Lane Extension and the Convent. O.C. 2 Section will have the guns of the Fort, Convent Lane, Ecluse Trench, and The Lock.

8. A receipt will be given for all trench stores etc and copy sent to C.H.Q. after relief.

9. Separate Orders to Transport Officer.

10. All billets, dugouts, emplacements, cookhouses, latrines will be personally inspected by Section Officers before relief, and left scrupulously clean.

11. On completion of relief, wire "NITA".

                                         (sd) S. Scott, Lieut,

                                          123rd Machine Gun Company.

In the Field,
   April 3rd 1916.

To.
1	War Diary	6	Transport Officer	9	124th M.G.Coy
2	Duplicate	7	123rd Infantry Bde	10	Xth C.M.G.O.
3	O.C. 1 Section	8	122nd M.G.Coy		
4	Os.C. 2 and 4 Sections				
5	O.C. 3 Section				

123 M.G. Coy
Vol 12

WAR DIARY or INTELLIGENCE SUMMARY

Army Form C.2118

Instructions regarding War Diaries and Intelligence Summaries are contained in F.S. Regs., Part II. and the Staff Manual respectively. Title Pages will be prepared in manuscript.

(Erase heading not required.)

Place	Date	Hour	Summary of Events and Information	Remarks and references to Appendices
Reninghelst	1		5 O.R. proceeded to Cookery Course Abeele.	
	2		Relieved 124 M.G. Coy in St Eloi Sector.	O.O.41.
Vöormegele	3		{Trench Troops.	
	4			
	5			
	6		1 Sgt proceeded to 2nd Army Rest Camp.	
	7		5 O.R. returned from Scouting Course.	
	8		Lt. S. Scott proceeded on Tactical Course, XIV Corps. Lt. A. Reid assumed command.	
	9		Very heavy bombardment of our lines about 9.10 pm	
	10		3 N.C.Os proceeded to Corps M.G.O. Course, Steenvoorde.	
	11		1 O.R. returned from A.A. Course.	
	12		Lt. S. Scott returned to Coy & resumed command.	
	13		1 O.R. returned from Sanitation Course.	
	14		{Trench Troops.	
	15			
	16		3 N.C.Os returned from M.G. Course, Steenvoorde.	
	17			
	18		{Trench Troops.	
	19		Lt. Hanson & Harvey returned from M.G. Course. Carriers & leave to UK respectively.	
	20		Relieved by 122 M.G. Coy in making Lt. S. Scott proceeded to Camiers on M.G. Course.	O.O.43.
Reninghelst	21		Coy engaged in cleaning, reorganizing & preparations to make for reinforcements.	
	22		1 Sgt proceeded to 2nd Army Rest Camp.	
	23		Fatigue party 50 O.R. to Abeele.	
	24		Lt. Graves 1 O.R. proceeded on leave. 1 O.R. proceeded on Cookery course.	
	25		Fatigue party to Abeele. 3 N.C.Os proceeded on reproducing ek course Abeele.	
	26		Batt. Horse Show. 3 Successes for Coy.	
Vöormegele	27		Relieved 122 Coy in St Eloi Sector. 12 O.R. from Inf. Bttns attached to Coy.	O.O.45.
	28		Lt. Hanson proceeded on leave to U.K. Bombardment of G.H.Q. & R. Lines 9-10	
	29		Heavy shelling round Voormezeele. 1 men of this unit killed in fort.	
	30		Trench Troops. 1 O.R. proceeded on leave.	
	31		Relieved by 122 M.G. Coy in St Eloi Sector.	

Army Form C. 2118.

WAR DIARY
or
INTELLIGENCE SUMMARY

(Erase heading not required.)

Instructions regarding War Diaries and Intelligence Summaries are contained in F. S. Regs., Part II. and the Staff Manual respectively. Title Pages will be prepared in manuscript.

Place	Date	Hour	Summary of Events and Information	Remarks and references to Appendices
			General	
			Throughout the month the m.gs of this unit have employed offensive tactics, firing many thousands of rounds by day & night on enemy communication dumps etc, in cooperation with Artillery. By night guns have been mounted on the front line parapets & fired at the enemy front line, supports & wire. There has been much enemy shelling. Voormezeele receiving daily attention, until it is almost obliterated now. A particularly long turn (18 days) in the trenches under these conditions tries every body very much. Advantage has been taken, to a considerable extent, of vacancies for courses on machine gunnery, map reading sanitation, cookery etc. 9-2 Sergeants have been sent to the 2nd Army Rest Camp for periods of 14 days. Leave has been reopened & 2 Officers & 2 O. Ranks were granted leave.	

June 1st 1917.

C D Upjohn
Major.
Commdg. 128. M. G. Company.

No. 1. War Diary

Operation Orders by Lieut S. Scott,
commanding 123rd Coy, M.G. Corps. (No.41).

Ref. 123rd Infantry Bde O.O.8, Warning Order No.7, and G.674/39.

1. The 123rd M.G. Coy will relieve the 124th M.G. Coy in the St Eloi Sector on the night of the 2nd - 3rd May 1917.

2. Sections will move off from the Transport Lines in succession, at intervals of half-hour, commencing at 8.30 pm.

3. Sections will take up positions in line as under:-

			Position	
Section 1	on left	Team 1.	L.B.6	Bus House trench (Old No.10)
		2.	L.B.7	Shelley Lane
		3.	L.B.8	Old French T, (Old No.12)
		4.	L.B.9	Oosthoek Farm
Section 2		5.	L.B.1	P & O T, (Old No.6)
		6.	L.B.3	Crater Lane
		7.	L.B.4	)
		8.	L.B.5	) Bus House
Section 3		9.	L.B.2	Moated Grange
		10.	L.B.14	Wheel House
		11.	L.B.16	Convent Wall
		12.	L.B.17	Convent Lane Extension
Section 4		13.	L.B.15	Fort
		14.	L.B.18	School
		15.	L.B.22	L. Scottish Wood
		16.	L.B.26a	R. Scottish Wood

"L.B" signifies "Left Brigade".
Section Headquarters are as follows:-
        No.2 Crater Lane R. Line
           1 Canteen   )
        3 & 4 Canteen Post) Voormezeele.

4. One guide per team from 124th M.G. Coy will meet incoming teams at old C.H.Q. Voormezeele, with the exception of the 2 teams for Scottish Wood which will be met at the corner of the road leading to Scottish Wood from Café Belge - Voormezeele Road.

5. Each Section will take its 2 fighting limbers, allotting in succession, one half limber to each gun team, in which all guns, tripods, gun kit, and packs will be placed.
Each man must take his load quickly, and take one pack. Packs, if not correct can be sorted out at gun position.
Limbers will move off as soon as cleared, by the Vierstraat - Kruisstraat road with the exception of No.8 limber which will return via Scottish Wood and pick up the relieved teams' guns etc.
Each Section must clear away from C.H.Q. before another Section draws up.

6. All trench stores, and 10 belt boxes per gun will be taken over, checked, and signed for by the Section Officers. A signed list will be sent to C.H.Q.
C.Q.M.S. 123rd Coy, will set aside 160 belt boxes, filled, to be handed over to 124th Coy, if required.

7. Quebec Camp will be left in a scrupulously clean condition. Pte Hamber, R.A.M.C., will inspect all latrines, cookhouses, tents, huts etc, before 7 pm, and report on their cleanliness to the Adjutant.

8. The C.Q.M.S. will issue rations for the 3rd May to every man before 6 pm on the 2nd.

9. Men will take one blanket each into the trenches. All spare blankets must be made into Section rolls, labelled and handed into Q.M. before 9 am, 2nd May.

10. On completion of relief wire "PROSERPINE".

11. Acknowledge.

        (sd) A. McKie. Reid, Lt & Adjt
        123rd Machine Gun Company.

Distribution

1. War Diary
2. File
3. O.C. Section 1
4.   " " 2
5.   " " 3
6.   " " 4
7. Transport Officer
8. 123rd Infantry Brigade
9. 124th Infantry Brigade
10. 124th M. G. Coy
11. Xth Corps M.G.O.
12. D.M.G.O.

Secret

War Diary

Operation Orders 43, by Lieut S. Scott,
commanding 123rd Machine Gun Company.

Ref. 123rd Inf. Bde O.O.85.

1. The 123rd Coy M.G.C. will be relieved by the 122nd Coy M.G.C., in the St Eloi Sector on the night - 19th/20th May.

2. One guide per gun team will report to old C.H.Q. at 11 pm, 19th inst, with exception of guides for Scottish Wood guns who will wait at junction of Scottish Wood - Cafe Belge road.

3. Sections will be relieved as under:-

    Section 3 (Right)   Commencing 11 pm, 19th.
    "   4 (Left)   "   11.30 pm, 19th.
    "   1 (Scottish Wood, Fort, School)
                            Commencing 12 pm, 19th.
    "   2 (Outer Defences, Voormezeele).
                            Commencing 12.30 am 20th.

4. Section Officers, on relief, will hand over all trench stores, R.E. stores, and ten belt boxes per gun, and will render usual certificates to H.Q. Tripods will not be handed over.

5. The limber of the last Section of 122nd Coy will carry away the four guns of No.3 Section 123rd Coy, on relief. The two Scottish Wood guns will be carried away by the limber of 122nd Coy which brings up the relieving guns to Scottish Wood. The remaining guns will be carried out by Transport of 123rd Coy M.G.C. One limber per section with the exception of No.3 Section as above.

6. The Transport will move back to Company Camp via, ELZENWALLE - BRASSERIE - RIDGEWOOD - HALLEBAST - MICMAC.
Each gun team on relief will move back independently under the gun team commander to RENINGHELST CHURCH. One man will be left with each limber.

7. All gun positions, dugouts, latrines, etc, will be left in a scrupulously clean condition. L/cpl Taylor, R.A.M.C. will be detailed to visit as many positions as possible during the day.

8. All men will carry their blankets strapped on their backs.

9. All clinometers and wiring gloves will be handed in to C.H.Q. before relief.

10. Separate Orders are issued to Transport Officer.

11. On completion of relief, wire "ROSEMARY".

12. Acknowledge.

(sd) A. McK. Reid, Lt & Adjt
123rd Machine Gun Company.

18th May 1917.

To. 1 War Diary
    2 File
    3 O.C. Section.1
    4   -do-   2
    5   -do-   3
    6   -do-   4
    7 Transport Officer
    8 O.C. 122nd Coy M.G.C.
    9 123rd Infantry Bde.
   10 Xth Corps M.G.O.
   11 122nd Infantry Bde.
   12 D M G O.

Operation Orders 45 by Major C.F.Dingwall
commanding 123rd Machine Gun Company.

Ref. 123rd Infantry Bde O.O.87.   Map 28.N.W. and 28 S.W.

1. The 123rd Machine Gun Coy will relieve the 122nd M.G. Coy in the St Eloi Sector onnight of 26th/27th May.

2. The 123rd Coy will arrive at Voormezeele in Sections at half hour intervals commencing 11 pm. Guides from 122nd Coy will be at old G.H.Q. at that time, with the exception of one guide for left Scottish Wood gun who will be at corner of road from Scottish Wood and Cafe Belge - Voormezeele road at 10 pm.

3. Sections will be disposed in the line as under :-

    No.1 Section on Left Sub-sector   L.B. 6, 7, 8 and 9.
     2   "   on right   "   L.B. 1, 3, 4 and 5.
     3   "   Voormezeele Defences   L.B. 2, 14, 16 and 17.
     4   "   " & Scottish Wood.   L.B. 15, 18 and 22.

4. Sections will parade at Transport Lines, ready to move off, as under:-

        Section No.1 9 pm   26th inst
           "   2   9.30 pm   "
           "   3   10 pm   "
           "   4   10.30 pm   "

    All four guns etc of each Section will be packed in one limber. Sections will march in front of limber and will not halt in Voormezeele until arrival at old G.H.Q.
    The limber of No.4 Section will leave the gun for Scottish Wood at end of road leading thereto, and will return that way to carry back guns of 122nd Coy, unless warned to the contrary. Remaining limbers, as soon as guns have been dropped, will proceed back via Brasserie - Ridgewood to transport lines.

5. Rations for 27th, and breakfast rations for 28th will be issued to the Coy by the C.Q.M.S. before 8 pm on the 26th.

6. Fighting kit only will be worn.

7. The Camp will be left perfectly clean. L/c Taylor, R.A.M.C. will be detailed to go round all huts, latrines and cookhouses, and will report to the Adjutant before the Camp is vacated.

8. On completion of relief, wire "SYLVIA".

9. Acknowledge.

                                  (sd) A. McK. Reid, Lt & Adjt
                                       123rd Machine Gun Company.

In the Field,
    24th May 1917.

To.1 War Diary
   2 File
   3 O.C.1 Section
   4   " 2   "
   5   " 3   "
   6   " 4   "
   7 Transport Officer
   8 122nd M.G.Coy
   9 123rd Inf Bde.
  10 M.G.Officer Xth Corps.

Army Form C. 2118.

WAR DIARY
or
INTELLIGENCE SUMMARY

(Erase heading not required.)

Instructions regarding War Diaries and Intelligence Summaries are contained in F.S. Regs, Part II and the Staff Manual respectively. Title Pages will be prepared in manuscript.

/ 23 M G Coy
Vol 13

Place	Date	Hour	Summary of Events and Information	Remarks and references to Appendices
Reninghelst	June 1.		Rest Billets at Quebec Camp	
	2.		Rest Billets	
	3.		-do-	
	4.		Rest Billets. Major C.F.Dingwall to U.K. (Auth A.G's A.6864) Lieut.Reid assumed command. Lt.r.C.O. Berkeley joined from the Base Relieved 122 M.G.Coy in St.Eloi Sector 8 guns to Battle Positions 1 Section with 20th D.L.I., 1 Section on Barrage. Relief complete by 3 am on the 5th.	O.O/48.
	5 & 6		Completing arrangements for the attack.	
	7		Attack on 2nd Army Front. Brigade attacked from St.Eloi Sector. Zero 3.10 am, attack successful. 8 guns with positions in Blue Line in front of Dammstrasse. 4 guns into Red Line, 4 guns on Barrage under 4th Corps M.G.O. Lieuts.Berkeley, Harvey & Russell-Jones wounded, 4 O.Rs killed, 13 O.Rs wounded.	
	8		C.H.Q. to No.5 Crater. Guns consolidating positions. 2/Lt Agate wounded.	
	9		Lieut.S. Scott returned from M.G. course, Camiers, and assumed command (Auth A.M.1318 dated 28.5.17). Lt Henson returned from leave to U.K.	
	10		Trench troops, holding & consolidating line. Heavily shelled by enemy. Lt Henson slightly wounded - remained at duty. 2 O.Rs wounded.	
	11&12		Relieved by 124 M.G.Coy.	O.O. 46 & map atted:
	(13,14		In rest at QUAKAKARKEHOLD FRENCH TRENCH	
	15		2/Lt F.R. Epton joined from Base.	
	16		In rest at OLD FRENCH TRENCH. 2/Lt J.H.Hyslop joined from Base	
	17		-do- 2/Lts.J.B.Jarrett & G.H.Johncox	
	18		-do- joined from Base.	
	19			
	20		Relieved 122 M.G.Coy in Left Brigade sector. 8 guns in line, 8 guns on Barrage. 3 O.Rs wounded.	O.O.49
	21		Trench troops	
	22&23			

Army Form C.2118.

WAR DIARY
or
INTELLIGENCE SUMMARY

(Erase heading not required.)

Instructions regarding War Diaries and Intelligence Summaries are contained in F. S. Regs, Part II. and the Staff Manual respectively. Title Pages will be prepared in manuscript.

Place	Date	Hour	Summary of Events and Information	Remarks and references to Appendices
Voormezeele	June 24		Inter Section relief	
	25		Lieut S. Scott wounded. Lt. A. McK. Reid assumed command.	0.0.50
	26		Trench troops. Heavily shelled. Enemy aeroplane brought down by our Anti aircraft machine guns. 2 O.Rs wounded.	
	27		Trench troops. 1 O.R. killed.	0.0.51
	28		Inter Section relief. 1 O.R. killed 3 O.Rs wounded.	
	29		Trench troops. 1 O.R. killed 3 O.Rs wounded.	
	30		Trench troops. preparations for relief by 47th Division.	

General Remarks

This month has been particularly eventful in the history of the Coy. The Company took a part in the attack on the WYTSCHAETE - MESSINES ridge. The Company distinguished itself. The Barrage fire under the Corps M.G.O., in which 4 guns co-operated, was wonderfully successful and effective as evidenced by intelligence from captured Germans. For several weeks previous to the attack, intense machine gun harassing fire was done by our guns, co-operating with artillery shoots. An average of 50,000 rounds per night was fired by this Coy alone for over a week.

For their gallantry in the active operations, three immediate awards have been given to the Company

No.27472 Sgt J. Horridge.   Bar to M. Medal.
No.14557 L/c S. Cooper.   Military Medal.
No.30356 Pte E. Curtis.

Authority Xth Corps R.O. No.1190 dated 27.6.17.

The Coy was unfortunate in losing Major Dingwall who went to M.G.T.C. on June 3rd, who had commanded the Coy for 7 months, and in losing Lieut.Scott who was wounded on June 25th and who had assumed command on returning from Camiers M.G. course on 9th inst.

The period of holding the line after the attack was particularly trying, as weather conditions allied to the terrific shelling of the enemy has told on the physique and morale.

WAR DIARY
or
INTELLIGENCE SUMMARY

(Erase heading not required.)

Army Form C. 2118.

General Remarks (continued).

During the attack and the following period of holding the line, the casualties were as follows :-

Officers wounded	6
O. Ranks "	28
O. Ranks killed	7
Total	41

A. McKie Reid. Lieut

Commanding 123rd Coy, Machine Gun Corps.

Field.
1.7.1917.

Operation Orders 48 by Lieut A. Mc.K. Reid,
commanding 123rd Machine Gun Company.
----

1. The 123rd M.G. Coy will relieve the 122nd M.G. Coy in the St. Eloi Sector on the night 4th/5th June 1917.

2. Sections will be disposed in the line as under :-

   No. 4 Section   L.B.9   Oosthoek Farm
                        L.B.8   Old French Trench
                        L.B.7   Shelley Lane

   No. 2 Section   L.B.6   Bus House Trench
                        L.B.4)
                        L.B.5) Bus House.

   No. 1 Section   L.B.14   Convent Lane (Wheel House)
                        L.B.22   Left of Scottish Wood.

3. Guides will be at the C.H.Q., Voormezeele at 12 midnight with the exception of the Scottish Wood guide who will be at the end of the road to Scottish Wood at 1 am.

4. Sections will parade at Transport Lines, ready to move off, as under :-

   No. 4 Section   9.30 pm
   No. 2 Section   10 pm
   No. 1 Section   10.30 pm.

   The three guns etc of each Section will be packed in one limber. Sections will march in front of limbers. As soon as guns etc have been dropped, limbers will proceed back via BRASSERIE - RIDGEWOOD to Transport Lines.

5. 10 filled belt boxes, and all trench and R.E. stores will be handed over. Tripods will not be handed over.

6. C.H.Q. will be in Old French Trench near L.B.8.

7. No.3 Section will remain in Quebec Camp tonight and will report to O.C. 20th D.L.I. tomorrow at a time to be arranged by the Section Commander with the O.C. 20th D.L.I.

8. Rations for the 5th will be issued to the Company by C.Q.M.S. before 9 pm on the 4th inst.

9. Fighting kit only will be worn. Packs will not be carried and will be dumped at C.Q.M. stores before Sections leave.

10. On completion of relief, wire "TINA".

11. Acknowledge.

                                             (sd) F.L. Shaw, Lt & A/Adjt,

                                                123rd Machine Gun Company.

In the Field.
4th 5.1917.

To.
    1   War Diary
    2   File
    3   O.C. Section.1
    4   -do-   2
    5   -do-   3
    6   -do-   4
    7   Transport Officer
    8   122nd M.G. Coy
    9   123rd Infantry Brigade.

SECRET

Operation Order No.46, by Major C.F. Dingwall,
commanding 123rd Machine Gun Company.

Ref. Maps - Sheets 28 N.W.)
            Sheets 28 S.W.) 1/20,000
----

1. **Preparation**
   The Second Army will have all preparations ready to attack by the 31st of May.

2. **Disposition**
   The 41st Division will be disposed as follows:-

   <u>On the right</u>   124th Infantry Brigade
                       1 Section 237th Field Coy, R.E.

   <u>On the left</u>   123rd Infantry Brigade
                       1 Section 233rd Field Coy, R.E.

   <u>Divisional Reserve</u>
                       122nd Infantry Brigade
                       228th Field Coy, R.E.
                       233rd Field Coy, R.E. (less 1 Section)
                       237th Field Coy, R.E (less 1 Section)
                       19th Middlesex Regt   (Pioneers)

3. <u>Days previous to attack</u>

   The attack will take place on Zero day
   Zero day will be referred to as Z day, and the preceding 5 days as Y, X, W, V, U.
   Days before "U" day will be known as Z minus 6 etc.
   Days after Z day as A, B & C.
   Days after "C" day as Z plus 4 etc.

4. <u>Frontage of Brigade attack</u>

   The 123rd Brigade frontage will be from a point 50 yards east of the left edge of Triangular Wood to a point 100 yards S.S.E. of Shelley Farm (map attached to Section Officers' copies).

   <u>Disposition of Battalions</u>
      11th Batt The Queens (Royal West Surrey Regt) on the left
      10th Batt Royal West Kent Regt,   in the Centre
      23rd Batt Middlesex Regt   on the right.

   The Brigade will be in position 2 hours before Zero. Each Battalion will form up in 6 waves. The procedure of the attack is shewn in the 123rd Infantry Brigade operations, and will not be reprinted here.

5. <u>Machine Guns</u>
   4 guns of the 123rd Infantry Brigade will be attached to the Divisional Machine Gun Officer for Xth Corps barrage.
   This battery will consist of 1 Officer detailed in Appendix I.
                       2 guns from No.1 Section
                       1 gun from No.2 Section
                       1 gun from No.4 Section.
   This leaves 12 guns available for the Brigade and will be distributed thus:-
       1 Officer and 2 guns of No.1 Section to 10th R.W.Kent Regt.
       1 Officer and 3 guns of No.2 Section to 23rd Middlesex Regt.
       1 Officer and 3 guns of No.4 Section to 11th Queens.
   The nominal detail of these teams will be issued later in Appendix II.
   Each gun team will be manned by 1 gun team Commander, 4 Machine Gunners and 6 Infantry carriers. The remainder of N.C.O's and men of these Sections will remain at Transport Lines under Lt. ~~Scott~~ Reid as reinforcements. See Appendix III.

- 2 -

The guns will move up with the last wave of each Battalion. H.Qs of the Section Officer will be at the respective Battalion H.Qs.
Each officer will take 1 runner and 1 batman, who will act as runner if needs be.
On the DAMMSTRASSE being taken, guns will be pushed out in front to resist counter attacks; the placing of these will be left with the officers and gun team Commanders. Each gun team will take 14 boxes of belt ammunition and 1 S.A.A. box in bulk.
Each gun team Commander and machine gunner, except Nos.1 and 2 will take 1 bandolier S.A.A.
At Zero plus 10 min these guns will form a barrage on to the Black Line and 500 yds behind until 3 hrs 40 min when the 122nd Infantry Brigade advance on to the Black Line see Appendix IV. Enough belt ammunition will always be kept handy to resist a counter attack.
Barrage fire will be opened by the Section Officers at any moment on instructions given him by the O.C. Battalion.
Section Officers and Gun team Commanders will keep careful watch for enemy field guns.
An infantry escort will be detailed for these guns.

Support Guns

6. 4 guns will be in support of the Brigade and will move up with the 8th wave.
These guns will be of No.3 Section and will be manned by one officer and the same number of personnel as for the attacking guns.
On arrival at the enemy support trenches the officer will place his guns into the following strong points which will be made by O.C. 20th D.L.I :- O.3c 4.0; O.3c 8.3; O.3d 3.5; and O.3d 65.70.
Detail for personnel of support guns will be found in Appendix V. These guns will resist all strong counter attacks should the attacking Battalions fall back.

7. Accessories
A mine will be exploded in the vicinity of the craters at Zero hour. Tanks will also be used. All Officers and N.C.Os will read the 123rd Infantry Brigade orders as soon as possible.

8. H.Qs 123rd Company, Machine Gun Corps will be at 123rd Infantry Brigade H.Qs at about I.32c 10.70.

9. All Section officers and gun team commanders will all be fully acquainted with their positions.

10. Remainder of positions for personnel will be found in Appendix 6.

11. Acknowledge, please.

(sd) .F. Dingwall, Major
Commanding 123rd Machine Gun Coy.

May. 30th 1917.

To. No.1 War Diary
    2 File
    3 2nd In Command
    4 O.C. 1 Section
    5 " 2 "
    6 " 3 "
    7 " 4 "
    8 Transport Officer
    9 123rd Infantry Bde
   10 11th Queens
   11 23rd Middlesex
   12 10th R.W. Kents
   13 20th D.L.I.
   14. Xth C.M.G.O.
   15 Spare

123rd Machine Gun Company.

Administrative instructions for forthcoming operations to be read in conjunction with
    41st Divn Administrative Instructions
    123rd Inf Bde   -do-   -do-
    123rd Inf Bde Operations Orders and
    123rd M.G. Coy Operation Orders.

Ref. Maps   28.N.W.   28 S.W.   1/10,000.

----

1. **Personnel**   As laid down in
    Appendix I   (Barrage personnel)
    Appendix II   (Attacking personnel).

2. **Reinforcements**
    These will remain at Transport Lines under Lt Reid, see Appendix III.

3. **Prisoners of War**
    All prisoners of war captured by machine gunners will be handed over to the Infantry for evacuation.

4. **Battle Stragglers**
    The line of the BOLLAR: BECK between Brigade bounderies will be patrolled by Regimental Police detailed from the Infantry to prevent straggling.

5. **Rations**   Rations for X day will be carried up on the man on the night of W/X.
    Rations for Y & Z days are dumped in the emplacements at Canteen Post (I.31c 30.80)
    The supply of rations for A day may present considerable difficulty. It is therefore of the utmost importance that every man should be in possession of a serviceable iron ration on "Z" day in the event of it having to be consumed on A day.
    Ration men from each gun team will be sent down at 7 am on "Y" day. As far as possible iron rations should be collected from casualties, and local reserves of rations made.
    A small piece of chewing gum will be issued to each man. It is found that if taken about half an hour before Zero hour it greatly helps to alleviate hunger and thirst.

6. **Water**   Every man will go up to the line on the W/X night with his water bottle full.
    Water for Y and Z days will be dumped with rations in Canteen Post.
    It is important that water bottles should be full on Y/Z night.
    Section Officers will obtain all information available as regards additional sources of water supply in their own Sectors.
    After the advance all ground must be searched for wells and other sources of water supply. Any such ground will be reported as soon as possible in order that arrangements may be made to test the water, which, must on no account, be used until declared fit to drink by the Medical Authorities.

7. **Medical**   Regimental Aid Posts
    No.1 At I.32d 1.1
    No.2 at I.32c 50.05.
    Wounded will be evacuated as far as possible by arrangement with Infantry stretcher bearers and R.A.M.C. stretcher bearers.

7. **Medical** (continued)

On no account is a gun team to be weakened in order to assist in the evacuation of wounded.

8. **Ordnance**
   1. The Divisional Ordnance Store will remain as at present at G.34d 65.35.
   2. The normal procedure of supply of Ordnance material will continue.
   3. All captured war material will be sent back at once to Divisional Ordnance.

9. **Ammunition**
   1. The forward ammunition dump of this unit is in a small copse at O.3a 3.7. There will be 200,000 rounds S.A.A. at this point. This amount will be maintained if possible.
   2. The advanced Brigade dumps are at I.31d 5.9
   I.32d 25.25
   3. Supply of ammunition from Divisional Dump to Brigade dumps will be by first line transport of units to Voormezeele, thence by tramway to dumps.

10. **Burials** As laid down in 41st Division Administrative Instructions.

11. **Veterinary**
   1. The mobile Veterinary Station will remain at its present position at G.33c 00.15.
   2. An advanced Veterinary Dressing station for wounded animals will be established at a farm at M.6b 15.90 (sheet 28) from the first day of bombardment, V day.

12. **Communications**
As laid down in 41st Division Administrative Instructions. Voormezeele - Shelly dump system of tramways will be used by this Brigade.

13. **Traffic Control**
As laid down in 41st Division Administrative Instructions.

14. **Trench Tramways**
As laid down in 41st Division Administrative Instructions. See Communications.

15. **First Line Transport**
This will remain in its position, ready to move at 2 hours notice.

16. **Sanitation**
   1. The greatest care must be paid to Sanitation. All troops, whether situated in the firing line or in the rear must invariably make provision for latrines.
   2. The indiscriminate fouling of the ground by using shell holes, as was done on the captured area last year on the SOMME, must be carefully guarded against.
   3. Special steps must be taken to guard al food from flies and rats.

17. **Salvage.** Whenever possible, parties and individual men returning from the front line must carry back some salvaged article with them.

18. **Baths and Laundry**
will be carried on as usual.

19. **Recreation** Soldiers Clubs, Y.M.C.As and Church Army Huts at Reninghelst, Dickebusch and Chippewa, are open to all troops.

20. **R.E.Stores** As laid down in 41st Division Administrative Instructions.

21. <u>Reports and Returns</u>.

  Section Officers will report as soon as possible
through Battalion runner system to O.C.123rd
M.G.Coy, C/o Brigade.
Reports should include.

   Disposition (Map,ref if possible)
   Operations
   Information regarding enemy, country water etc
   Casualties
   Strength of Teams
   Requirements, etc.

Other reports will be sent as often as possible.

       (sd) A. McK.Reid, Lt & Adjt
        123rd M. G. Coy.

31.5.17.

To. 1. War Diary
  2 Duplicate
  3 2nd in Command
  4 O.C.1 Section
  5 2
  6 3
  7 4
  8 Transport Officer
  9 123rd Infantry Bde
  10 Spare.

Dispositions of guns of 123rd Coy. M.G.C. immediately after attack of 7-6-17.

Legend:—
Machine Gun...... △
Anti Tank Empt... ⊡
Strong Point....... ⋈
Wire
Battle Position...
Barrage Guns......
Reserve...........

Message

..........DIVISION.
Map reference
or Mark on Map
at back.

1. My {Company / Platoon} has reached................
2. My {Company / Platoon} is at............... and is consolidating.
3. My {Company / Platoon} is at............... and has consolidated.
4. Am held up by M.G. at...............
5. I need :— Ammunition.
   Bombs.
   Rifle Grenades.
   Water.
   Very lights.
   Stokes shells.
6. Counter attack forming up at...............
7. I am in touch with............... on Right at...............
                                     on Left
8. I am not in touch with............... on Right
                                         on Left
9. I am being shelled from...............
10. I estimate my present strength at............... rifles.
11. Hostile {Battery / Machine Gun / Trench Mortar} active at...............

Time............ m. Name...............
Date..................... Platoon...............
                           Company...............
                           Battalion...............

Operation Orders 89 by Lieut. S. Scott,
commanding 123rd Machine Gun Company.
----

1. The 123rd M.G. Coy will relieve the 122nd M.G. Coy in the Left Bde Sector 41st Div front on night 20th/21st inst.

2. Sections will be distributed as follows:-
   Section.1   a. O.11a 1.9   Opal Trench
   Right Subsector   b. O.10b 8.8
                        c. O.4c 6.2   Oak Trench
                        d. O.4c 7.3

   Section.3   a. O.5c 3.3
   Left Subsector   b. O.5c 6.7
                        c. O.5c 4.8
                        d. O.5c 1.5

   Section 2. Barrage guns at O.3d 55.25,   EIKHOF FARM

   Section 4. Barrage guns at O.3b 95.95,   CANAL BANK

3. Guides will be at crossing of railway over OESTHOEK ROAD
   For guns for Oak Crescent (Section.1)   at 8.15 pm
   For Sections 2 and 4   at 6.   pm

4. Only 6 men per team will be taken exclusive of Sergeants. Team will carry gun, tripod, spare parts box, oil box, 2 boxes belt and 1 petrol can of water to positions. Clinometers will be taken by Sections 2 and 4.

5. All trench stores and belt boxes will be taken over from 122nd M.G. Coy and a receipt given for same. A list of such stores will be sent to C.H.Q.

6. Rations for 21st will be drawn before leaving and carried into the line by teams.

7. Coy H.Q. after relief will be at LOCK HOUSE, SPOIL BANK.

8. Separate orders are issued to T.O. and C.Q.M.S.

9. All dugouts, cookhouses, latrines etc now used by the Company will be left in a scrupulously clean condition. L/Cpl Taylor, RAMC, will be detailed to visit all these before 6 pm and report to Headquarters on completion.

10. On completion send "TINA".

11. Acknowledge.

                                (sd)   A. McK. Reid, Lieut
                                       For O.C. 123rd Coy M.G.C.

19.6.1917.

To.   1. War Diary
      2. Duplicate
      3. O.C. Section.1
      4.   -do-   2
      5.   -do-   3
      6.   -do-   4
      7. O.C. 122nd M.G. Coy
      8. H.Q. 123rd I. Bde
      9. H.Q. 122nd I. Bde.
      10. Xth Corps M.G. Officer.

Operation Orders 50 by Lieut S. Scott,
commanding 123rd Coy, M.G. Corps.

1. Sections 2 and 4 will relieve Sections 1 and 3 respectively on the night 24th/25th June.

2. 2 Teams Section 2 will relieve the 2 teams of Section 1 at O.4c 65.15 (OAK CRESCENT). On completion of relief, the remaining 2 teams of Section. 2 will relieve teams of Section.1 at OPAL RESERVE trench.
   The relieved Section (Section.1) will take over the barrage positions at EIKHOF FARM.

3. On completion of relief, Section 2 will be under the command of 2/Lt Johncox.

4. Section 3, on completion of relief will take over barrage positions at O.3b 95.95 (CANAL BANK).

5. All trench stores, anti aircraft duties, arcs of fire etc will be handed over.

6. Guns, tripods, belt boxes etc with the exception of spare parts boxes will be handed over and receipts given and received.

7. On completion of relief send "URSULA".

8. Acknowledge.

(sd)   A. McK. Reid, Lieut,
For O.C. 123rd Machine Gun Company.

In the Field,
23.6.17.

To.   1. War Diary
       2. Duplicate
       3. O.C. Section.1
       4.   -do-   2
       5.   -do-   3
       6.   -do-   4
       7. H.Q. 123rd Inf Bde.

Operation Order 51 by Lieut A. McK. Reid.,
commanding 123rd Machine Gun Company.
----

1. Sections 1 and 3 will relieve Sections 2 and 4 respectively on night of 28th/29th. Time to be arranged by Section Officers concerned.

2. Gun teams will take up their original positions.

3. Section Officers will see that 10 belt boxes per gun are in each position. All surplus to be returned to C.H.Q. at once.

4. Section Officers will report to Battalion Commanders of their Sectors as soon as possible after relief.

5. All particulars regarding fields of fire etc <u>must</u> be handed over by Gun Team Commanders.

6. Guns, tripods, belt boxes etc, with the exception of spare parts will be handed over.

7. Anti aircraft and barrage schemes will be handed over by Os.C. 1 and 3 to Os.C. 2 and 4.

8. On completion of relief, send "VERITY".

9. Acknowledge.

                                        (sd) M.J.V. Hanson, Lieut

                              For O.C. 123rd M. G. Company.

In the Field,
27.6.17.

```
To. 1  War Diary
    2  Duplicate
    3  O.C. Section.1
    4     -do-      2
    5     -do-      3
    6     -do-      4
    7  Headquarters 123rd Bde.
```

Army Form C. 2118.

WAR DIARY
or
INTELLIGENCE SUMMARY

(Erase heading not required.)

123 MG Coy
Vol 14

Instructions regarding War Diaries and Intelligence Summaries are contained in F.S. Regs., Part II. and the Staff Manual respectively. Title Pages will be prepared in manuscript.

Place	Date 1917	Hour	Summary of Events and Information	Remarks and references to Appendices
Old French Trench	July 1		Relieved by 142 M.G.Coy in the forward gun positions	O.O. 52
	2		Relieved by 140 M.G.Coy in the Barrage positions.	O.O. 53
Murrumbidgee Camp	2		Company marched from Murrumbidgee Camp to the BERTHEN area. Coy billet at Sheet 27 S.E., Q.34b 4.5 near THIEUSHOUK. Coy marched very well.	
THIEUSHOUK	3		Rest billets	
	4		—do— Gun cleaning.	
	5		—do— Gun drill, limber washing & gun cleaning.	
	6		—do— Gun drill, spare parts inspection. 4 O.Rs proceeded to Map reading course at ABEELE.	
	7		—do— Limber washing, Company close-order drill. Communication drill for N.C.O's. Mechanism, Gun drill, Lecture on Indirect fire. 2 Officers and 2 O.Rs attended lecture at BERTHEN on "Aeroplane co-operation with Infantry".	
	8		—do— Church Parade at C.H.Q., 1 Officer granted leave to U.K.	
	9		—do— Saluting drill, route march., Lecture on A.A. defence	
	10		—do— Saluting drill, gun drill, mechanism, stoppages: Company Close-order drill. 1 O.R. to Gas Defence course, BERTHEN. 1 O.R. to A.A. course. 4 O.Rs retnd from Map reading Course.	
	11		—do— Limber washing, gun drill. Inspection by Divnl Commdr who expressed himself highly satisfied with the Coy's turn out. 5 Medal ribbons were presented to the Coy. Lieut. T.H.L. Turner reported from the Base as 2nd in Command.	
	12		—do— Saluting drill, kit inspection, gun drill, T.A.I O.R. proceeded to U.K. on leave. 1 Officer & 3 O.Rs attended lecture on "Aeroplane photographs".	
	13		—do— Saluting drill, revolver practice, route march, 1 Officer & 3 O.Rs attended lecture at BERTHEN on "Gas". Inspection of billets by G.O.C. 123rd Infantry Bde.	
	14		—do— "Threes" drill. Coy played the 20th D.L.I. in Football Competition — result 0 - 6.	
	15		—do— Brigade Sports. Coy succeeded in getting 3rd in Relay Race.	
	16		—do— Saluting drill, close-order drill. No.2 Section proceeded with 23rd Middlesex for tactical exercises. Rest of Coy, Practical use of ground & cover. 18 men per Battn attached	

Army Form C. 2118.

WAR DIARY
or
INTELLIGENCE SUMMARY

(Erase heading not required.)

Instructions regarding War Diaries and Intelligence Summaries are contained in F. S. Regs., Part II. and the Staff Manual respectively. Title Pages will be prepared in manuscript.

Place	Date	Hour	Summary of Events and Information	Remarks and references to Appendices
	1917 July			
THIEUSHOOK W	17		Rest Billets	
			No 2 Section paraded with 20th D.L.I. for Tactical, exercises, and No.2 Section with 23rd Middlesex. Remainder, & Transport, revolver practice. G.O.C. inspected attached men, and returned 25 of them as unfit for the work. The Company held a Concert in the evening.	
	18		Sections paraded with Battalions for Tactical exercises.	
	19		Gun cleaning, limber washing. Gun drill & spare parts inspection.	
	20		Coy close-order drill. No.4 Section paraded with 11th Queens.	
	21		Company marched from BERTHEN area to WESTOUTRE area. Company marched very well, no men fell out.	O.O.54
WESTOUTRE	22		Rest billets. Cleaning up after march. Church parade.	
	23		-do- Kit inspection. Guns and spare parts inspection., limber washing.	
	24		Relieved 124th M.G.Coy in "BLUFF" Sector. H.Q. at Bluff Tunnels. 2/Lieuts. Epton, Acason, Johncox, Hyslop & Jarrett in the line, Lt.Shaw in reserve in LARCH WOOD.	
	25		Trench troops. Cpl Arculus missing, 2 O.Rs killed, 5 O.Rs wounded.	
	26		-do- 1 O.R. killed, 2 O.Rs wounded.	
	27		-do- 1 O.R. wounded	
	28		-do- Considerable rain.	
	29		-do- Cpl Arculus reported killed.	
	30		Attack in Bluff Sector, N. of YPRES - COMINES Canal. 2/Lieuts., Acason, Epton, Jarrett, & Hyslop each took 3 guns in the attack at 3.50 am. Owing to the extremely bad weather conditions the guns became quickly useless except for firing single shots. Three guns which got into dugouts were able to be cleaned, and 2 of them obtained targets during the counter attack on the night of July 31st. One of 2/Lieut Epton's guns did considerable execution on the enemy moving about on the edge of a wood. Our casualties were: 2/Lt Hyslop wounded, 4 O.Rs killed, 1 O.R. missing, 21 O.Rs wounded.	

Army Form C. 2118.

WAR DIARY
or
INTELLIGENCE SUMMARY

(Erase heading not required.)

Instructions regarding War Diaries and Intelligence Summaries are contained in F.S. Regs., Part II. and the Staff Manual respectively. Title Pages will be prepared in manuscript.

Place	Date	Hour	Summary of Events and Information	Remarks and references to Appendices
			GENERAL REMARKS	
			The period in rest for the first 3 weeks of the month was spent in excellent weather. Sports, football, concerts etc, were held for the benefit of the troops. Unit training and training with the Infantry Units in the attack was carried out. The last week was a particularly strenuous one, for the holding of the line in the days previous to the attack was done under trying conditions of weather, accomodation, and enemy activity. This comparatively long, and strenuous period - 6 days - during which the troops were in the line previous to the attack, did much to lessen the nerve and energy so essential to attacking troops.	

Arthur Reid Captain

Commanding 123rd Machine Gun Company.

Operation Orders 52 by Lieut A. McK.Reid, M.C.
commanding 123rd Coy, M. G. Corps.

Ref. Map, Sheet 28.   Ref 123rd Inf Bde. O.O.100.

1. The 123rd M.G.Coy will be relieved on July 1st, and night of July 1st/2nd, and to be completed by 3 am July 2nd.
The 142nd M.G. Coy will relieve the 8 guns in front of the DAMSTRASSE.
The 140th M.G.Coy will relieve the Barrage guns at EIKHOF FARM and the CANAL BANK.

2. Guides   One guide per gun team from the 8 forward guns (Sections 1 & 3) will report to the H.Q. of the 142nd M.G.Coy at the Power Station (Concrete Dugout) in the DAMSTRASSE at 3 pm on the 1st inst.
One guide from each group of Barrage guns (Sections 2 & 4) will report to C.H.Q. in OLD FRENCH TRENCH at 1.30 pm on the 1st inst. Sections Officers of 1 & 3 Sections will select guides who know the Power Station. The guides, if necessary, will reconnoitre the route beforehand.

3. Sections will hand over 10 filled belt boxes per gun, all bulk ammunition, and all information regarding field of fire, anti aircraft defence, neighbouring guns etc to relieving teams. Section Officers will hand a signed receipt of all stores etc handed over to C.H.Q. on completion of relief.

4. On completion of relief Sections will report to C.H.Q., and will proceed thence to MURRUMBIDGEE CAMP (N.7a 5.8) on the LA CLYTTE - RENINGHELST road, about 500 yards from LA CLYTTE, under Section Officers.
One man per gun team will remain at C.H.Q. to accompany the guns on the limbers.

5. All emplacements, dugouts, latrines etc will be handed over in as clean a condition as possible.

6. Separate Orders are issued to the Transport Officer.

7. Acknowledge.

In the Field,   (sd) M. J. V. Hanson, Lieut
   30th June 1917.   For O.C. 123rd Company, M.G. Corps.

To.   1. War Diary
      2. Duplicate
      3. O.C. 1 Section
      4. O.C. 2 Section
      5. O.C. 3 Section
      6. O.C. 4 Section
      7. O.C.140th M.G.Coy
      8. O.C. 142nd M.G.Coy
      9. Headquarters 123rd Bde.
     10. Xth Corps M.G. Officer.

Operation (March) Orders 53 by Lieut A. McK. Reid, MC
commanding 123rd Coy, M.G. Corps.

Ref. Maps Sheet 27 & 28 Hazebrouck 5A.
Ref. 123rd Inf. Bde O.O. 101.

1. The 123rd M.G.Coy will proceed from MURRUMBIDGEE CAMP to the
BERTHEN area on July 2nd.

2. The Company will be ready to move off from MURRUMBIDGEE CAMP by
1.30 pm, July 2nd, and will march via RENINGHELST & GODEWAERSVELDE
to THIENSBROUK (at Q.34b 4.4).
The Transport will move in rear of the Company.

3. The limbers will be packed during the morning of the 2nd, after
clothing parade which will be at 8.45 am.
Limbers are allotted as under.
All gun stores etc in fighting limbers - each Section complete
in its own two limbers.
    A & B Limbers   - C.Q.M.S. Stores
    C   Limber   - at O.C's disposal
    D   Limber   - Transport Stores (chaff cutter, corn
                                mill etc) & Pioneers'
                                kit.
    H.Q. Limber   - Fore Portion - Orderly Room stores.
                      Rear Portion - Rations & dixies.
All bulk forage will be carried in hay nets and feed bags.
C.Q.M.S. will detail Pte Berry to tie all spare dixies under
limbers.
All Officers' kits and mens' packs will be carried on their own
Section limbers if other transport (G.S. wagon) is not available.

4. Dress   Fighting kit, haversacks on back. Mess tins with covers
slung from haversacks, waterproof sheets under flaps of haversacks.
Steel helmets will be carried on the left shoulder. Box
respirators will be carried.
All water bottles will be full.

5. One man will walk behind each limber as brakesman. These will
be detailed by Os.C. Sections, and C.S.M. for 'letter' limbers.

6. No man may fall out without permission from an officer.

7. The Company will march in threes. March discipline will be
maintained. There will be a halt from ten minutes to each hour
until the hour.

8. Acknowledge.

                                          (sd) M.J.V. Hanson, Lieut
In the Field,   For O.C. 123rd M.G. Company.
1.7.1917.

To.
    1. War Diary
    2. Duplicate
    3. O.C. Section 1
    4.   -do-   2
    5.   -do-   3
    6.   -do-   4
    7. Transport Officer
    8. C.S.M.
    9. C.Q.M.S.
   10. 123rd Inf Bde
   11. Xth Corps M.G.O.
   12. Spare.

Operation Orders (March) 5't by Captain A. McReid, M.C.
Commanding 123 Coy M.G.C.

1. The 123rd M.G. Coy will move from the Berthen area to the Westoutre area on 21st July.

2. The Coy will be ready to move off from C.H.Q at 9.30 am and will march via Godewaersvelde and Boeschepe.

3. Transport will move in rear of Coy.

4. Limbers will all be packed by 7.30 am, 21st July. Limbers are allotted as under:-

All gun stores etc in fighting limbers - each Section complete with its own 2 limbers

      A & B limbers - C.Q.M.S. stores
      C   " - O.C's disposal
      D   " - Transport stores (chaff cutter, corn mill etc) & Pioneers' stores
      H.Q. " - Fore portion - Orderly Room stores
               Rear " - Cooks' stores etc

All bulk forage will be carried in hay nets & feed bags. C.Q.M.S will detail Pte. Barry to tie all spare dixies <u>under</u> limbers. Mens' packs will be on limbers - officers' kits on lorry.

5. Dress - Fighting kit, haversacks on back, mess tins with **covers** slung from haversacks, w.proof sheets under flaps of haversacks. Steel helmets will be carried on left shoulder. Box respirators will be worn; water bottles will be filled.

6. One man will walk behind each limber to act as brakesman. These will be detailed by Os. C. Sections, & C.S.M. for 'letter' limbers.

7. No man may fall out without permission from an officer.

8. Acknowledge.

(sd). M.J.V. Hanson, Lt & Adjt
123. Coy, M.G. Corps.

20.7.1917.

To 1. War Diary
2. Duplicate
3. O.C. 1. Sect.
4. " 2 "
5. " 3 "
6. " 4 "
7. Transport. O.
8. C.S.M.
9. C.Q.M.S.
10. 123 Inf. Bde
11. 4th Corps M.G.O.
12. Spare (O.C.)

C O P Y.

Army Form C. 2118

WAR DIARY
INTELLIGENCE SUMMARY

123rd. M.Gun Coy.,
August, 1917.

Place	Date Aug. 1917.	Hour	Summary of Events and Information	Remarks and references to Appendices
BLUFF SECTOR.	1.		Consolidation of line was continued after attack of 31st.July. The weather conditions were very bad, and state of ground rendered movement very difficult. A large number of casualties were inflicted by enemy snipers, and in consequence Lt.HYSLOPE was wounded. Eight guns remained in the line at)a.6.a.50.30. 0.6.a.35.80. I.36.b.40.25. I.36.b.45.75.)a.6.a.40.50. I.36.c.60.10. I.36.b.45.30. I.36.b.50.95.	
	2.		The remaining 4 guns were out of action owing to mud & the impossibility of cleaning them without dry shelter, and these were brought down to H.Q. in the BLUFF TUNNEL. Weather continues bad.	
	3.		Company relieved in the line by 124 Coys. and comes back to ELLENWALLA to rest, 2nd.Lts.Jarrott, JOHNSON sick, and Lt.ALASON? to Corps Rest Station.	
	4.		Men attend baths.	
	5.		Cleaning kit.	
	6.		Company relieves 124th. Coy.in the line, 8 guns in 4 gunson barrage at "B" Battery position.	
	7.		Shelling less severe.	
	8.		2 guns from railway embankment moved back to BUFFS BANK.	
	9.		Positions chosen in BATTLE WOOD for one gun and at I.36.a.40.60. for 2 guns which are occupied by 3 of the barrage guns under Lt.Shaw.	
	10.		Coy. relieved in the line by 124 Coy. & moved back to RIDGE WOOD. Casualties during tour in the trenches 8 O.R. Killed 1 officer& 29 O.R. wounded. 1 O.R. missing 6 gassed.	
METEREN.	11.		Move in motor lorries to X4c44 near METEREN.	
	12.		Kit inspection.	
	13.		Gun kit cleaned.	
	14.		Gun drill. T.of E.T. of new draft.	
	15.		Inspection by Corps Commander.	
	16.		Route March, Gun cleaning. 2/Lts.EPTON & HANSON take 8 guns and 2 sections to ABEELE on anti-craft work.	
	17.		The brigade was inspected by G.O.C. II Army. 2 Anti-air craft guns were mounted on the parade ground.	
	18.		Church Parade.	
STAPLES.	19.		The Company marched to STAPLES.	
ESQUERDES.	20.		" " " " ESQUERDES.	
	22.		Cleaned up equipment and gun equipment. Bathe in the river. 2/Lt.WOOD joins the Company.	
	23.			

Captain, ? H. Coy, 2nd.Echelon.

Army Form C. 2118.

123rd. M. Gun Coy.
August, 1917.

C O P Y.
WAR DIARY
or
INTELLIGENCE SUMMARY.
(Erase heading not required.)

Instructions regarding War Diaries and Intelligence Summaries are contained in F. S. Regs., Part II. and the Staff Manual respectively. Title pages will be prepared in manuscript.

Place	Date	Hour	Summary of Events and Information	Remarks and references to Appendices
ESQUERDES.	AUG.1917.			
	23.		The Company fired Part II Table C on the range at Q.35.a.3.5.	
	24.		The Division was inspected near LAFOSSE FARM by the Commander-in-Chief.	
	25.		Training commences. 2/Lts.MULHERN & REED jlin the Coy.	
	26.		Church Parade.	
	27.		Training .Battery Drill for Barrage work occupies a large portion of the training time.	
	28.			
	29.		(signed) A.MC KIE REID., Capt.,	
	30.		Commanding 123rd. Coy., M. Gun Corps.	
	31.		Capt. REID commences M.G. course at CAMIERS.	

CERTIFIED "TRUE COPY":-

[signature]
Capt.,
G. H. Qrs.,3rd. Echelon.

WAR DIARY or INTELLIGENCE SUMMARY

Army Form C.2118.

123rd COY. M.G.C.

September 1917.

Place	Date	Hour	Summary of Events and Information	Remarks and references to Appendices
Eecquedeques	1		Inspection of clothing, gun stores, etc.	
	2		Sunday - Rest Day	
	3		Sections practiced the attack with the Brigade. Particular attention paid to dispersing the guns in line nearing formation after gaining the objective.	
	4		Firing on the range at Inglingham. No. 3 & 4 Sections returned to the Coy from Abeele where they had been engaged on A.A. work.	
	5		Barrage firing in the morning. Preliminary meet of Brigade sports in the afternoon.	
	6		Brigade Sports considering the size of the unit the boy did exceptionally well.	
	7		Brigade operations practising in advancing in support of attack that has been checked. Sections co-operated, the remainder representing the frontage & the enemy. Divisional Horse Show. The boy won the mule race. Lt. George Smith acting O.C. broke his collar bone in the Point-to-Point. 2nd Class shown "30 ft D.P."	
	8			
	9		18 m/m a peculiar as carried from 33 in Middl "30 ft D.P."	
	10		Sunday - Rest Day	
	11		Coy Firing Chiefly barrage work. Training of attached men.	
	12		Pay Day. C.O. returned from Camiere School	
	13		Gas demonstration & testing of gas helmets by Divisional Gas Officer. Lt. Turner evacuated to England.	
	14		Rifle firing on range at Lumbres. Gramophone concert in the evening.	
Staple	15		Coy marched from Eecquedeques to Staple. The Brigadier complimented the Coy	
Meteren	16		Coy marched from Staple to Meteren.	
Reninghelst	17		Coy marched from Meteren to Reninghelot (Ontario Camp)	
	18		Preparations for forthcoming attack.	
Ridge Wood	19		Coy moved up to Ridge Wood with exception of fighting limbers. Nos. 1 & 3 Sections moved to Zevel Farm at 28 Midnight	
			No. 2 & 4 " " " Hedge Street Tunnels " 11th evening	
Shrewsbury	20		Coy moved up to Hedge Street Tunnels.	
Forest			Attack on the Ypres - Zanebeke Ridge at 5.40 am. The moncell erbered.	
			Moved up to Zevel Farm. In the evening No. 4 Section moved up to Bodmin Copse with 11th Queens. No. 1 Section employed by O.C. 17th Bodmin Copse.	
			2nd Rd. Wood with 16 O. Ranks referred to by O.C. word to protect batteries on barrage work. He took over 4 of their guns.	
	21		The 123rd M.G. Coy made an up to 15th oppose the following Section moved up guns up to 15th oppose the Zevel Farm 16 gives was maintained in	
			Shelling around the attack. Lt. Langon (No. 4) at 9.30 am. Lt. Langon (No.4 casualties incurred	

WAR DIARY or INTELLIGENCE SUMMARY

123rd M.G. Coy
for September 1917
Army Form C. 2118

Place	Date	Hour	Summary of Events and Information	Remarks and references to Appendices
Thryonhay Forest	22, 23		41st Division relieved in the evening. The Coy attached to the 39th Division at 6pm. Nos 1 & 3 Sections took over "C" Battery from the 62nd M.G. Coy. 2 Lt. Spots acting as Battery commander. Nos 2 & 4 Sections took over "D" Battery from the 61st M.G. Coy with 2Lt Jardon as Battery commander.	
	24		During the evening orders came in from the D.M.G.O. 39th Divn to the effect that we were to carry out barrage for the next attack. The C.O. supplied out the figures during the night.	
	25		Before the enemy made a counter attack. Despite heavy shelling "C" Battery did and both No. 2nd Section were relieved at "C" Battery by 228 M.G. Coy moved to 2D Battery on the left of "C" Battery (T.25a.ma.70) all day was spent on improving nice positions & erecting aiming posts, etc.	
	26		Our 2nd moved to a central dugout to act as group commander.	
		5.50 am	The new attack was launched. Our 2 batteries fired for 1/2 hr. but as they were finishing the enemy reflied heavily on the right Battery. 2/Lt Mulholm & C.O. Banks were killed & 2 wounded. 2 guns were blown up. The Coy was relieved at 7am by 114 M.G. Coy & got out of the line without casualties.	
Reninghelst	27		It moved back to from Camp, Reninghelst.	
	28		Stocktaking & refitting with clothes.	
	29		Transport moved off at 9.a.m. to travel to La Panne via Abeele Herzeele, Crombouck, Wylder Bergues-Dunes. They had orders to stay the night at Crombouck.	
Bray Dunes	30		The Coy moved in 6 buses to Bray Dunes via Crombouck & Bergues. The transport reached Bray Dunes at night.	

A. McKenzie Captain
commdg: 123 M.G. Coy.

Army Form C. 2118.

WAR DIARY
or
INTELLIGENCE SUMMARY OCTOBER 1917

(Erase heading not required.)

123rd M.G.C. Coy.

Instructions regarding War Diaries and Intelligence Summaries are contained in F.S. Regs., Part II. and the Staff Manual respectively. Title Pages will be prepared in manuscript.

Place	Date	Hour	Summary of Events and Information	Remarks and references to Appendices
BRAY DUNES	1		Cleaning Guns and Limbers. Bathing.	
	2		Cleaning Guns. Barrage Drill. Gas Drill. Bathing. 2/Lt. McNeil posted to No 1 Section. 2/Lt.Guyatt posted to No 2 Section.	
	3		Cleaning Limbers. Checking Stores. Bathing. 2/Lt.Turpin joined Company Attached men from Middlesex & Durham Light Infantry rejoin their units.	
	4		Close Order Drill. Mechanism, I.A. Lecture on Barrage. 2/Lt.Turpin posted to No 4 Section.	
COXYDE BAINS	5		Company marched to COXYDE BAINS via LA PANNE. Arrived 1.30 p.m. and take over Billets. Captain Reid Acting "." M.C.O. 41st Division. Lieut.Hanson and 15 O.R. go to reconnoitre new positions in the NIEUPORT BAINS Sector.	See O.O.61.
	6		Cleaning Guns and Limbers. Inspection of Gas Masks. Transport move to new lines in COXYDE BAINS. 2/Lt.Epton, McNeil and Guyatt, and Sgt. Avis reconnoitre new position in line.	
NIEUPORT BAINS SECTOR	7		Company relieved the 127 Coy: in the NIEUPORT BAINS Sector. No 1 Section - R.Front Sub-Sector - 2/Lt. McNeil. No 2 " - L. " " - 2/Lt. Guyatt. No 3 " - 2 Coast Guns & 2 Guns in reserve - 2/Lt.Epton. No 4 " - under 2/Lt.Turpin in reserve at Transport Lines, COXYDE BAINS. 1 Section of 124 Coy: in reserve position under 2/Lt. Knight. Relief complete by 12.30 Midnight 7-8th October. Captain Reid hands over to new D.M.G.O.	See O.O.62
	8 9 10 11 12 13		During these days the Company whilst in the line were engaged in improving the Emplacements,tunnels and trenches. All the positions were for defence and with the exception of a little Anti-Aircraft work, no firing was done. Lieut.Shaw left the Company for 6 months Light Duty in the U.K. (Auth: XVth Corps A.C/8738. A.809 (O.1) d/- 4.10.17.)	
	14		Military Medal awarded to Sgt.Oates and Pte.Sutton - Ref.D.R.O. 2242 d/- 13.10.17	

Army Form C. 2118.

123rd M.G. Coy.

WAR DIARY
or
INTELLIGENCE SUMMARY OCTOBER 1917.

(Erase heading not required.)

Instructions regarding War Diaries and Intelligence Summaries are contained in F.S. Regs., Part II and the Staff Manual respectively. Title Pages will be prepared in manuscript.

Place	Date	Hour	Summary of Events and Information	Remarks and references to Appendices
COXYDE BAINS	14		The Company relieved in the line by 124 Coy: Relief complete at 3.15 a.m. 15.10.17. The Relief was carried through satisfactorily and the Company moved into billets at COXYDE BAINS. There were no casualties during the whole time in the line.	See O.O.63.
LA PANNE	15		The Company moved off from COXYDE BAINS at 2.0 p.m. for LA PANNE, stopping at ST.IDESBALD on the way for Baths. Arrived LA PANNE and took over billets. Draft of 12 men under L/C.Duffield met the Company at LA PANNE.	
	16		Cleaning and checking Gun stores, etc. 2/Lt.Williams joined the Company and Posted to No 2 Section.	
	17		Baths at St.Idesbald. Barrage Drill.	
	18		Gas Drill. Action from Limbers. Barrage Drill.	
	19		Anti-Aircraft Drill. Indirect Fire and Barrage Drill.	
	20		Inspection by C.O. Route March to ADINKERKE. 2/Lt. Mc Neil and 2/Lt.Williams attend Demonstration of A.A.Sights at Divnl. Headquarters, ST IDESBALD. Sergt.Moore J. awarded D.C.M. for Gallantry in the Field 20.9.17. (Ref.D.R.O.2268 d/- 20.10.17.	
	21		Sunday - Rest Day. Lieut.W.Hannah transferred from 97th Coy.M.G.C. to take over position of 2nd in Command. Auth: 41st Div.wire No A613d/- 17.10.17	
	22		2/Lt.Guyatt attended course of Artillery at 190th Artillery Brigade, H.Qrs. I.A. Gun Drill. Indirect Fire & Barrage Training.	
	23		Firing on the beach cancelled owing to rain. Work carried on in Billets.	
	24		Company fired stoppages on the Beach.	
	25		2/Lt.Williams, Sgt.Stone and Cpl.Mettock attend a course at LA PANNE on Anti-Aircraft Defences. The C.O.attends Demonstration of Barrage fire	

Army Form C. 2118.

123rd M.G. Coy.

WAR DIARY
or
INTELLIGENCE SUMMARY

OCTOBER 1917

(*Erase heading not required.*)

Instructions regarding War Diaries and Intelligence Summaries are contained in F.S. Regs, Part II. and the Staff Manual respectively. Title Pages will be prepared in manuscript.

Place	Date	Hour	Summary of Events and Information	Remarks and references to Appendices
LA PANNE	26		Barrage Drill. Gun Drill. Revolver Drill.	
	27		T.O.E.T. Revolver Drill. Company & Section runners attend Signalling Course under 1/Cpl.Major.	
	28		Company training carried out - Gun Drill, Use of ground and cover, and practice in building emplacement on sand dunes.	
	29		Checking of Company Stores - Completing to Mobilization Strength, etc.	
	30		Route March - LA PANNE - ADINKERKE - ZEEPANNE PLACE - LA PANNE. 3 Hours.	
	31		Cleaning limbers.	

During this month only 7 days were spent in the line, the remainder of the month being spent in training out of the line. Much useful work was done in the way of Barrage Fire training and Indirect Fire generally. Stoppage practices were fired on the beach on two occasions and considerable practice in the principles of open warfare has taken place.
On the earlier days of the month, before the company went into the trenches, practically the whole company bathed daily in the sea - a beneficial and pleasant recreation.
There have been no casualties during the month and few sick.
36 O.R. and 1 Officer went on leave to U.K. 16 of the former were recalled for the 30th in view of a Divisional move.
Three new officers, 2/Lts.Guyatt, Williams and Turpin joined the Company A considerable number of officers and O.R. went to various courses.
All horses were clipped, but mules were not clipped owing to their penchant for chewing the horse rugs. The establishment of animals is at last complete.
Generally the month has been satisfactory for the progress of the Company.

Ankin Res
Captain
Comm'g. 123rd M.G.Company.

www.ingramcontent.com/pod-product-compliance
Lightning Source LLC
Chambersburg PA
CBHW081549160426
43191CB00011B/1881